PEACE OF MIND

More than ten years ago, Dr Ian Gawler, a veterinarian and decathlon athlete, used meditation to help overcome his own cancer which had been diagnosed as terminal. Since then, he has assisted thousands into a personally satisfying experience of meditation. This book is the fruit of that experience.

A large part of Ian Gawler's work is shared with his wife, Gayle, conducting the Melbourne Cancer Support Group for the Australian Cancer Patients' Foundation. At the Living Centres, through residential and ongoing sessions, the Gawlers' programmes help patients and families to mobilise their own resources. These programmes which incorporate the meditation methods set out in this book have brought fresh hope and renewed health and peace of mind to many while inspiring the formation of a network of other active, self-help groups. There have been many remarkable recoveries.

In 1987, Dr Gawler was awarded the Order of Australia Medal in recognition of his service to the community.

PEACE OF MIND

HOW YOU CAN LEARN TO MEDITATE AND USE THE POWER OF YOUR MIND

DR. IAN GAWLER O.A.M., B.V.Sc.

AVERY PUBLISHING GROUP INC.

Garden City Park, New York

By the same author
You Can Conquer Cancer

ISBN 0-89529-447-8

CONTENTS

For my children,
Rosemary, David, Peter and Alice

Go with the Flow

Be still like a Mountain
Flow like a River

ACKNOWLEDGEMENTS

Naturally, many people have made significant contributions to this book. Gayle and the children have parted with my company on many occasions and I thank them for their love, support and understanding. Gayle has been involved and added to every phase of this work.

Without Dr Joan Humphreys' astute corrections and typing, and wry wit, this book would have been years longer in the doing. Similarly, I also thank my publishers for their help; Michael Zifcak for helping to make some of the proceeds from the book available to The Australian Cancer Patients Foundation; Michelle Anderson for her sense of humour and enthusiasm; Susan Gabor and Letty Gregory for their editing.

My understanding of meditation has grown through contact with many people and books. The latter are mostly listed in the reading list given at the end of this book. The people include Rayner Johnson (his lectures and book *The Imprisoned Splendour* awakened me at an early age to a view of reality that I felt I already knew but had somehow forgotten), the late Dr Ainslie Meares, Peter Hoddle, Norma Pelic, Sai Baba, Paul Solomon, Professor Chris Magarey and Siddha Yoga, Zen Master Hogen and many who have shared Christian Meditation with me must also be thanked for shared knowledge and insight.

This book is really the product of helping so many people learn to meditate. I am indebted to them all, for their shared experiences, responses, feedback, failures and successes. It is a privilege to be able to work in this way.

And in particular I wish to thank my main fellow workers, David McRae, Eileen Bevidge, Robert Proctor, Angela Fergie and my friend Bob Sharples. Here I make special note of David McRae who takes a major role within The Foundation and enriches all he does with compassion, humility and love.

I express my appreciation to Rick Wallis for the frontispiece photograph. Thanks too, to Derek Hughes who combines sensitivity with his superb professional photography.

All these wonderful people and books have helped a great deal, but in meditation, the real answers lie within. I am deeply grateful for the experiences and the knowing that comes from listening and waiting in silence for that still small voice within.

AN INTRODUCTION

Greetings!

In opening this book you are joining the already vast and ever increasing numbers of people interested in learning to meditate. They are being drawn towards meditation as it becomes obvious that people who meditate regularly seem to have something 'special' in their lives.

It is often hard to pin down what this something is, but in my experience, regular meditators are characterised by increased efficiency in all aspects of their lives. Often they simply enjoy good health. Others have overcome significant illnesses. Their secret, the 'something special' in their lives, is that these people know the many benefits from experiencing Peace of Mind.

People who meditate are usually just plain, old-fashioned happy. And their smile comes from deep down inside.

To be happy is to be healthy, so, when you are serious about being healthy, it is time to learn to meditate.

Why start?

Perhaps stress has pushed you to the brink and you feel that one more crying child, one more demanding phone call, one more bill to pay, one more nerve-wracking day, will push you over the edge into a physical or mental breakdown.

Perhaps, quite simply, you feel life is lacking in zest. You wonder as to its purpose, you feel there is something missing in your life, you have an inkling that there is something more and you yearn to experience it.

Perhaps you are currently battling an illness and are looking for a way to help yourself – to create an ideal environment, inner and outer, in which your natural healing processes can work at their marvellous best.

Perhaps you are seeking to make friends with yourself, to get to know more about yourself: Who am I? Where am I going?

Perhaps you are seeking to find meaning in your life, to experience inner peace, well-being and real health, to realise your full potential.

For any or all of these reasons, when you are serious about taking an active part in your own health, it is time to take some time out and learn to meditate.

You will not have to drop out, cop out or give up the things you value in life. You will not have to burn incense, shave your hair, or even wear a kaftan! Just take some time out, relax physically, be still inwardly – *and learn to meditate.*

What is meditation?

If you have read a little already, or have asked a few people, you will realise it means many things to many people. So, what *is* meditation? It is remarkable how vague or evasive some are in actually defining it. This is almost certainly due to the fact that the verb, *meditate* is very similar in scope to the verb, *travel.* If you were setting out to travel up a mountain, for instance, you could choose to walk, ride a bike, catch a train or fly in a helicopter. You could set out from any number of starting points and presumably follow one of any number of paths that would eventually lead up to the same peak.

> Meditation is a process intended to lead to a direct
> experience of a higher level of consciousness.

Just as you could *travel* by walking or by flying a helicopter, you can *meditate* in different ways. When you begin any journey, you choose your mode of travel depending on your nature and your needs. So, too, with meditation.

This book intends to act as a traveller's guide to meditation – to point out the benefits of the destination and the options available as to how to get there. After reading it, you should feel confident and empowered to begin your journey.

What are the aims of meditation?

After asking many people their prime motive in learning to meditate, it is clear that the current upsurge of interest in it is because meditation is seen to provide a solution to the problem of satisfactorily meeting three great needs – stress management, self management of disease, and personal and/or spiritual development.

Traditionally, meditation was used as a tool for spiritual development. These days, the emphasis has been placed on its health-promoting qualities for in its simplest form meditation is an ideal stress management technique, and it also helps the body maintain, repair and heal itself.

To get the full picture of meditation's scope, I find it is useful to think of it as having three main paths, each of which has its own primary purpose and its own set of techniques. We will examine each in detail and then you will be free to decide which of these paths you wish to explore.

Meditation can be used as a pathway to health, insight and creativity.

Health Meditation

The theory behind Health Meditation is fairly simple:

(i) The body in its natural state of balance has a tremendous potential and ability to maintain and repair itself. In its natural and healthy state, the body's internal chemistry is in a condition of dynamic equilibrium – the hormones, blood components, heart rate, blood pressure, muscle tone, etc. are all ideally poised to maintain good health. So, if we cut a finger, the body is well equipped to heal it. The more complex process the body orchestrates when healing a broken bone is nothing short of a miracle. Similarly, the fact that the body can resist so many infections and maintain itself in so many different climates and conditions is quite marvellous.

(ii) The mechanisms involved in this self-regulating, self-healing process are well described as being the immune system. As long as the body's chemistry is in its normal state of balance, the immune system maintains good health.

(iii) When the immune system is not functioning normally, is not in balance, the body is not able to maintain and repair itself. It loses the capacity for self-regulation.

(iv) Stress is well-recognised as a major cause of upsetting the body's natural, internal, chemical balance. Stress impairs the immune system, and so lays the body open to disease.

(v) Health Meditation aims to produce a profound state of relaxation — physical and mental. In this relaxed state, a body whose internal chemistry has been unbalanced by stress, has a chance to regain that natural balance.

(vi) Health Meditation therefore counteracts the effects of stress. At the same time it creates an ideal internal state, an ideal balance in the body's chemistry, so that the immune system can function at its best.

(vii) In summary then, Health Meditation creates conditions in which the body's natural healing ability can work at its best. Health Meditation releases our own inner healer — gently and effectively.

In its simplest form, Health Meditation is best described as the Relaxation Response. This technique is easily learned and practised. It is a form of deep relaxation which rapidly and reliably brings immediate physical and psychological benefits.

The Relaxation Response is so important that we will spend several chapters elaborating on why it works and how to do it well. Basically, however, its methods are uncomplicated and easy to apply. Its whole emphasis is on its simplicity, naturalness and effortlessness.

Given its many benefits, I see the Relaxation Response as being a basic life skill — something that everyone should have the opportunity to learn, practise and benefit from.

As a part of Health Meditation, the Relaxation Response can lead on into a deeper mental stillness which, in fact, is an altered state of consciousness, just as to be asleep is to be in a different state of consciousness compared with when we are normally awake. This altered state is more a mystical state of consciousness. It is harder to define and describe to someone else. However, it does produce tangible gains in terms of added health benefits — physical, psychological and spiritual. This state is not so easy to enter as is the Relaxation Response, nor does practising it lead to such predictable results. However, those with the motivation, patience and perseverance are well rewarded, as going the extra step adds another dimension to our health and well-being.

Insight Meditation

Insight or analytical meditation is used as a means of discovering what is real. Getting to know yourself and your world. Really, what are your opinions, attitudes, beliefs? What are the answers to such questions as: Who am I? Where am I going? What is life all about? What do I want from life? What do I want to give? What do *I* want to do?

Of course, this type of analysis can be done on an intellectual level, too, by just thinking about it. The additional benefit of using Insight Meditation is simply that it can add profound insight. This can produce an exceptional clarity, a feeling of certainty concerning 'what is', and what your future direction should be. If you are interested in these benefits, the practice is worth the effort and hard work.

Insight Meditation's methods are based on a five-step process that invariably begins with learning how to concentrate selectively. To be able to hold the attention on one particular thing and to exclude distractions. This quality of selective concentration is well described as 'mindfulness' — the ability of our mind to hold its attention on what it chooses without forgetting it or wandering off on to other things. It is a state of discriminating alertness.

In this state of mindfulness you have the quality of being a very alert, impartial observer. Like someone watching and recording traffic going by on the highway. Being aware in great detail that, yes, that is a green Holden, a blue Ford, a 750 Kawasaki etc. — observing, but observing impartially, fully focussed on what is there, but not analysing, commenting, inferring or fantasising. In this state you are not saying, 'Wow! There goes a red Ferrari. Boy, I could just imagine myself in that, speeding down the highway!', but 'There goes a red Ferrari, and a blue Holden', etc. — simply recording what passes by.

The advantage of practising mindfulness is basically two-fold.

Firstly, it teaches us selective concentration. It is a good exercise in mind development. This ability to concentrate selectively is useful in all forms of meditation.

Secondly, mindfulness allows us to be more aware of 'what is'. It allows us to practise breaking free of old beliefs, habits and fantasies and to experience — to see what is actually there. As an impartial observer we can then approach each new situation as a fresh experience, free from past conditioning. We can act in an appropriate way for the moment rather than reacting in the same old habitual way. Mindfulness teaches us how to act consciously rather than to react subconsciously. We will discuss techniques specifically designed to practise and develop it.

This particular branch of meditation, Insight Meditation, has been well described as an opportunity to make friends with yourself. It is an active, mental process, not without its highs and lows. While it is an exciting path to personal discovery and can lead to states of higher consciousness, it requires concerted effort to practise. Its immediate physical health benefits are not generally as rapid or reliable in coming as are those with Health Meditation.

Creative Meditation

Creative Meditation provides an opportunity to consciously use the power of the mind.

We know, for example, how destructive the pointing of the bone can be in the aboriginal tradition. We know how constructive the placebo response can be. Clearly, what we think has a tremendous bearing on what we experience.

So Creative Meditation provides a mechanism to assist us in using our mental activity — to actively, creatively achieve our chosen goals. It has enormous potential and many pitfalls which, again, we will discuss in greater detail.

Its methods rely on an understanding of how the mind works and how we can work it — consciously. This is important as many of our actions in life are really reactions. We react to situations unconsciously, in a manner based on old habits. Often we are not happy with these old habits and are seeking a way to change them — a way to respond to new situations freshly, in a new and more appropriate manner.

Initially, making an effort to do this, to make changes in our life, involves a sense of effort, a wanting to make things happen. However, practised in conjunction with the simpler, more mentally passive Health Meditation, it soon develops a naturalness and allows us to use the full potential of the mind in an expanded, creative and useful way.

Bringing it together

Returning to the analogy of travelling up a mountain, it is as if there are three major 'stations' or destinations *near* the top of the mountain, named Health, Insight and Creativity. Each 'station' has a number of different paths leading up to it, and each path provides a different experience along the way. We can represent this diagrammatically:

The Pinnacle—The peak experience

It leads to
Harmony

It leads to
Mindfulness

It leads to
achieving
Chosen
Goals

This pathway
begins with the
Relaxation
Response

This pathway
begins with
Concentration

This pathway
begins with
Affirmations
and Imagery

**HEALTH
MEDITATION**

**INSIGHT
MEDITATION**

**CREATIVE
MEDITATION**

Not surprisingly, some meditation techniques range over two or even all three of these major pathways. For example, a specific meditation technique aiming to develop and achieve forgiveness may begin with a calming, stabilising form of Health Meditation, then encourage analysis of the situation through Insight Meditation, and finally, creatively generate feelings of forgiveness through Creative Meditation.

The pinnacle, the highest point in meditation, lies *beyond* the three stations. Thus, venturing up and on from any *one* 'station' leads to the same peak experience (pardon the pun!). The view from the top is the same, regardless of how you got there.

That peak experience is an altered state of consciousness characterised by a deeply relaxed body and a still mind. Now, to experience this stillness of mind is not to enter a nebulous void. In fact, it has a feeling of heightened awareness, of an acute sense of 'being here now'. The 'here' is a mystical place — a place that seems to be empty and complete all at the same time. Yet it is experienced as something very real. The feeling is of experiencing something very real, very dynamic, very precious, very comfortable and comforting. It is as if, over the past years, we have been seeing through a mist and now the mist has lifted.

To experience something tangible within this mental stillness is to know that there is a reality which lies beyond this body we live in, these emotions we feel and these thoughts we think. To experience this grand stillness is to have a sense of deep contentment. We know ourselves to be a valuable part of something much bigger than this frail body. We develop a sense of awe, and of order, and a gratitude for being here. We see Life as having a purpose and a meaning. Now, our trials, as oppressing as they may sometimes seem, also come into a new perspective. Seen from this new perspective, they too have their place. They are seen to be but transitory; we develop a confidence that they will pass and we will be the better for them.

The enduring reaction to experiencing this simple stillness is that everything is 'all right'. A profound quiet confidence in life, and in self, is generated. Peace of Mind is established.

The smile comes from deep down inside.

What can be gained from a book?

This is a practical book. It has been written with the intention of assisting you into a satisfying experience of meditation.

Firstly, is it real to expect to be able to learn meditation from a book? My belief has always been that the really worthwhile things in life should be straightforward and simple. That does not mean to say that they have to be easy – that is another matter. Worthwhile things usually take effort, patience and perseverance, but in essence they should be simple. Meditation is simple. In essence, it is very simple. Not easy – simple. And well worth taking seriously.

The aim of this book is to present meditation simply, in a way that allows it to be used as a true self-help technique.

There are many external things we will talk about that will help you in your meditation. A good teacher and a group to join in with are certainly helpful – not essential, but helpful. However, meditation is first and foremost an internal experience. It will be your experience – no one else can have it for you or do it for you. The benefits you gain will derive from the practice you actually do. Meditation is not something that I, or anyone else, can do for you. You will be in control. Meditation is a true self-help technique.

Meditation is a path you must travel yourself. The book aims to point the way, the safest and easiest way. It aims to throw light on the pitfalls, and to enthuse you to take the first step on the journey.

My own first guide to meditation was a book. Its directions were at best murky, and I fumbled around for quite some time. Since then I have read many more books and have been fortunate to meditate with many people and experience many different techniques. More recently, as a teacher, I have shared in the experiences of thousands of people as they began learning to meditate. From these people I have learned much about what worked for them, what they experienced, the problems or barriers they encountered and how they overcame them.

So my approach to meditation has always been pragmatic and eclectic. What interests me is what works. I trust that this book will be a suitable, clear expression of this accumulated experience and that, with it, you will be able to establish effective and rewarding meditation.

What of traditional meditation techniques?

In our modern Western context, people are coming into meditation with cultural and intellectual backgrounds that are very different from those who centuries ago took up any one of the major meditation paths, whether Christian, Zen, Sufi, Buddhist, or whatever.

This does not mean that these purist paths do not lay good claim to a valid place in our current society. But, clearly, the benefits of meditation are accessible now to many more than just those attracted to an ordered spiritual life.

Modern Western people can use their intellect to conceptualise the vast range of approaches to meditation and to the experiences recorded in meditation. This will provide a clear picture of what meditation is, how to do it, and how to overcome any obstacles that may be encountered.

From this base of knowledge I hope you will be confident and empowered to enter into this wonderful adventure.

How to use this book

To use this book, I suggest you read it through first. It is quite possible to learn to meditate well without direct guidance. Because I have shared with so many groups, you will find that most, if not all, of your questions will be answered.

If you can join a meditation group or attend a course, so much the better. Many people find that an extra advantage, but do be reassured by the knowledge that many have learned to meditate on their own.

Through the book we will explore the principles required for good meditation and the practices that can be used to achieve it. The conclusion will concentrate on what to do and provide a practical course of action, with options depending on your own experiences.

Be prepared to enjoy yourself! This is a great internal adventure, an exploration into the inner self, into the place wherein dwells truth, reality and the inner healer. So let's begin.

You **can** learn to meditate!

You **can** experience Peace of Mind.

Part One

STILL MIND

Chapter One

IN THE BEGINNING

How I began

My own involvement with formal meditation began following a major life crisis. Prior to this, throughout my university days at veterinary school, I had been drawn towards meditation. It felt like a good thing to do. The few books I read that touched on it fascinated me and I went to listen to visiting Indian leaders. But all the meditation courses at that time seemed to have a heavy Eastern flavour and the guru, beads and incense held no appeal for me. The images they conjured conflicted with my middle-class Christian background and, anyway, my spare time was preoccupied with training for the decathlon and enjoying other aspects of university and then veterinary life. Meditation became something I was keen to do 'one day'.

That day arrived in early 1975. Bone cancer, osteogenic sarcoma, was diagnosed in my right thigh. My leg was amputated through the hip. Faced with this crisis, I began to search for meaning and health and looked to meditation for answers.

To write the word *crisis*, the Chinese combine the hieroglyphics for *danger* and *opportunity*. Faced with this life crisis, the danger motivated me to do what I could to prevent my cancer returning, and the opportunity was there to learn all I could about life. In meditation I hoped to help my body maintain and repair itself while I discovered something of my own inner nature and reality.

I bought two books specifically on meditation, puzzled my way through them, adopted a course of action, a method, and determined to practise for thirty minutes each day.

I had no idea of what would happen. Nothing much did! Each day at 6 p.m., with very few exceptions, I would squat on the floor with my one leg crossed, put a hand on one knee, the other on an empty boot, close my eyes and try to concentrate on the tip of my nose.

After about nine months of this I had the experience of a beautiful, iridescent blue colour appearing before my closed eyes. When I tried to 'look' at it, or analyse it, it disappeared; when I did not think of it, it reappeared. On the few times that it did appear, I felt extremely comfortable — just plain good.

Then one day a white light appeared all around me. It was so vivid that I jumped and opened my eyes, thinking my wife, Gayle, had turned on the lights. She had not. It was pitch dark in the room! Something had happened, and this time it felt really good. Whoopee! I thought.

The next thing that happened was that my cancer reappeared. Curiously, the reappearance was not as might have been expected. Normally, when osteogenic sarcoma spreads, it goes into the lung tissue, but mine occurred in the lymph nodes inside my pelvis and chest, which seemed a little less threatening. I wondered if the meditation, crude as it was for me at that time, had had at least a little effect! Even so, I was expected to live for only three to six months.

So began an epic adventure. Gayle and I were convinced we could find a way to overcome this crisis and find a way to conquer cancer.

We tried everything, both conventional and unorthodox. Two and a half years later, with the help of many people and much personal effort from Gayle and myself, I was indeed found to be free of cancer.

Meditation proved a mainstay throughout that period. The first big step had been attending intensive sessions with Melbourne psychiatrist, the late Dr Ainslie Meares. For two months I attended his group sessions and gained a great deal. While I felt some considerable benefit, the cancer kept growing.

We then travelled overseas — the Philippines, India and Europe — learning and practising meditation all the time.

At the same time Gayle and I delved into all the self-help options, dietary considerations, positive thinking techniques, massage, natural healing methods and anything else that might have helped my condition. No desperation, no panic, just a concerted, fully committed search for what would work. All the time we drew on the inner reserves that meditation gave access to.

Finally, the combination of techniques began to work. The pieces in my jigsaw of health began to fit together. My old symptoms disappeared and a new pattern of health emerged. I took up my veterinary work again and we began a family. We now have four wonderful, energetic children.

A new beginning— The Melbourne Cancer Support Group

After going through that remarkable experience, Gayle and I felt we were in an ideal position to help others who were facing a similar major life crisis. We felt that while there were a lot of other people putting vast amounts of energy into researching and refining what the medical system could do for cancer patients, very little time was being given to what the patients and their families could do for themselves. It seemed to us that the role of the actual patients, their partners and other support people, was being neglected or completely overlooked.

Therefore, in 1981, Gayle and I, encouraged by Dr Meares, developed a twelve-week self-help programme and established the Melbourne Cancer Support Group. My book, *You Can Conquer Cancer*, published by Hill of Content in 1984, outlines the principles we build from in these groups. Meditation is the backbone of the programme, along with good food and creative thinking. It is an active programme, a combination of health education and mutual support that offers hope in a loving, caring environment. We also discuss pain control, death and dying, healing, the causes of cancer, positive attitudes and emotions, philosophy and stress management. More than two thousand people attended these sesssions during the first five years.

A lifestyle for health and well-being

More recently, it is heartening to observe that there has been an increasing urge amongst the public to take up a lifestyle of health. The thrust is not only towards preventing cancer and other degenerative diseases, but in actively seeking out peace of mind and well-being — to experience the best possible level of health. Many non-patients have read that first book and taken up our health-orientated principles, realising that the best way to conquer cancer is to prevent it.

More than this, our approach concentrates on living well. In so doing, it not only offers the prospect of preventing illness but it is a reliable path to a profound and sustainable level of health and well-being. So now, meditation is seen by many as being a key to health and well-being.

Learning and teaching meditation

In the support groups, and in the seminars I have conducted all around Australia, I have been fortunate in being able to help several thousand cancer patients and an even greater number of non-patients as they take their first steps into meditation.

My approach to meditation has always been a pragmatic one. I have been far more committed to results, to what works, than to any particular method or technique. I have aimed to translate the mysteries into something accessible and effective.

I have been fortunate in having close contact with so many people and being able to get feedback, to find out what they have experienced, what their hurdles were, and how they overcame them.

This book on learning to meditate, the result of their pooled experience and knowledge, is a tribute to each and every one of those wonderful people.

The cancer patients, and in particular their families, have taught me much. Many of them have had to face what is probably the ultimate health challenge of our time, cancer, and have come through it with a sense of victory. Not all of them lived, but that did not diminish their sense of pride or achievement in the way they responded to their situation. A growing number — about fifty at the time of writing — have recorded remarkable and medically unpredicted recoveries from what was thought to be terminal cancer. Others have found that being able to approach dying with a sense of dignity and well-being, being able to experience it as a peak — a meaningful conclusion to their life — has been victory enough.

Many others have taken joy in knowing that, through their own efforts applied within a comprehensive self-help programme, they have contributed significantly to the outcome of their own destiny. These people are positive that their own contribution, added to what was done for them medically, became a significant factor in their recovery. Many of these people, according to medical predictions, had perhaps a fifty-fifty chance of recovery and feel sure that their own efforts gave them the best chance of being in the right fifty. Just as importantly, once they got their All Clear, they felt confident that the programme they had adopted was their best insurance for a healthy future.

There are many moving stories to tell – dramatic stories of people who overcame other illnesses; subtler but equally powerful stories of people regaining balance, finding meaning and developing a new purpose and zest for living.

The benefits of meditation

So, why is it that people in such large numbers are learning to meditate? And what is in it for *you*?

Integrating meditation into your life will provide the answers you seek. How to live a full, active and effective life free from the effects of negative stresses. How to activate the complex and wondrous potential of your body to heal itself of the physical, emotional, mental and spiritual imbalances we call disease. How to have a rich and rewarding personal experience of spiritual reality.

To experience these sources of well-being, to experience them in your life as a reality, is well worth serious attention. It is worthwhile to approach meditation with a passion, a desire that burns as strongly as your desire for daily food, your desire for wealth, pleasure, happiness. Dare to be enthusiastic! Get excited and delight in it! Meditation could be the most wonderful personal experience you enter into.

Curiously, once fired by this burning desire, you will need to realise that meditation is only complete when the desire is itself transcended. In time, you will need to temper the aching need to 'do it right' and to move on, past the striving, to experience meditation in its completeness. Its completeness lies, finally, in doing it easily, effortlessly, without trying or striving, without desire – just simply doing it.

Learning a new skill

Firstly, realise that learning to meditate is very similar to learning to drive a car. It takes some motivation, some knowledge and practice and then the development of skill.

A little child begins life happily oblivious to the advantages of driving a car. Someone else attends to their needs, they get transported to and fro, life goes on and it's all very simple.

Then one day comes a dawning. The car is a key to travelling more freely in the world. If I take time to learn how to drive it, I will be able to move about, to take my friends with me and to use my time more effectively. So, by teenage years, most children are aware of the advantages of learning to drive. They know many others have done it, and they spend time and money to develop a new skill.

At first it's all in the head. What do I do first? Put the key in the ignition, turn it on, one foot on the clutch and the other on the accelerator, one in, one out, don't forget the indicator, and Pow! Off we go, bunny-hopping down the street. It's all in the head, consciously trying to think it through. No flow, no skill.

Practice moves us past the need for conscious thought. As we do it over and over, it starts to happen automatically, easily, effortlessly. So, after a little tentative practice and some cautiously gained experience, we can just get into the car and, without actually dwelling on it, start the car and drive it off — effortlessly.

If halfway through a journey a little girl ran out on the road in front of your car and you had to think: 'What do I do? Oh yes, one foot on the clutch, other on the brake', and so on, you would probably squash her! But, as an experienced driver, you can act swiftly and surely, without having to think about it. Now you have skill. You can just do it.

As an experienced driver, you will be able to travel across the busiest city, negotiate all manner of obstacles and potential hazards and arrive safely at your destination. On arrival, you will realise that you did not need to think about the method, the *how* of how you got there, you just did it. It all seemed so easy and natural.

So, too, with meditation. You need to begin with a burning passion for success, to plunge into it with all the enthusiasm of a major new learning experience. Then comes the development of understanding and of techniques — the learning, the practising, the conscious effort. Then the benefits begin to flow. With repetition, with practice, comes the flow, the ease.

Be aware of this process in gaining a skill. It will help you to be patient in learning to meditate. This normal progression in learning any new skill can be represented thus:

The four steps in learning a new skill

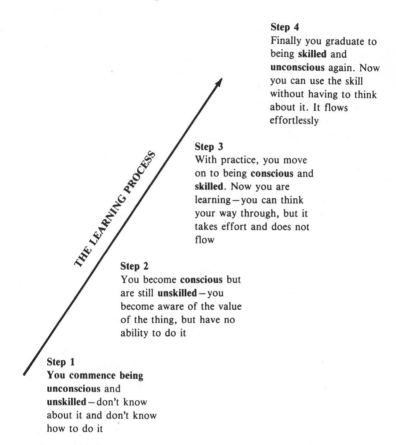

Step 4
Finally you graduate to
being **skilled** and
unconscious again. Now
you can use the skill
without having to think
about it. It flows
effortlessly

Step 3
With practice, you move
on to being **conscious** and
skilled. Now you are
learning — you can think
your way through, but it
takes effort and does not
flow

THE LEARNING PROCESS

Step 2
You become **conscious** but
are still **unskilled** — you
become aware of the value
of the thing, but have no
ability to do it

Step 1
**You commence being
unconscious** and
unskilled — don't know
about it and don't know
how to do it

Meditation—an effortless non-thinking skill

Being aware of this concept of using a skill knowingly, but in a non-thinking manner, is a great help when beginning to learn any form of meditation. It is especially important with Healing Meditation, for here we are aiming more specifically to experience stillness of mind. Dwelling on how we are going to do that, or thinking while we are actually doing it, obviously will prevent us from reaching the goal!

We cannot have an active mind and a still one at the same time! Now, this is no great mystery or trick. We are doing the same type of thing every time we drive the car. It is no problem to consciously practise beforehand, or to explain afterwards what we did. But, when it comes time to actually be doing it, we must just do it! No effort, no analysis, just do it.

Happily then, in meditation we can identify the skills we need to develop. Once we are aware of them, we can practise them until we can just do it — not think about it, not struggle or strive, just do it. Use the skills and experience the benefits.

It took me two and a half years of constant practice to realise the simple fact that the peak experience of meditation begins when everything else stops. In fact, there is really very little to do in order to experience it. It is a simple state where the body is deeply relaxed and the mind is still. We just have to let it happen.

But what do I do?

Not surprisingly, the simplicity of this is initially very difficult for some people. So often I hear, 'That's great. Sounds terrific — nothing to do, eh? But how do I do nothing? If I sit down and close my eyes all that happens is I think of all the things I haven't done. There's the garbage to put out, what's for dinner, what's on tomorrow, and hell, I forgot to pay that bill. Besides, my backside hurts!'

Hopefully the book will help you to appreciate what is required. Happily, there is a range of straightforward techniques designed to help you to do nothing!

There are other more analytical and creative techniques. All require practice and skill. The book is intended to enthuse you enough to practise and so lead you fairly rapidly into experiencing the delights of meditation. Also, please be clear that along the way there are many immediate benefits to be gained.

Chapter Two

THE PRINCIPLES OF MEDITATION

Let us seek now to deepen our understanding of what Meditation is and why it works. This is necessarily a trifle intellectual; how to do it is a lot more straightforward. Hopefully, this initial understanding will add more skill to your practice and you will find that it is worth the effort.

Levels of experience in meditation

Perhaps the most valuable thing I can offer from my contact with many meditators is the knowledge that to enter into meditation is not to leap off into some nebulous void. There are stages of experience in meditation which you are likely to meet and enjoy. The first stages are easily reached. They are very accessible and produce rapid, obvious and widespread benefits. To reach the higher levels requires diligence and perseverance, while the benefits of doing so are subtler but equally profound.

One of the common difficulties I encounter with people beginning meditation is that they have the concept that meditation means a still mind in a deeply relaxed body, and nothing else. They expect great benefits from achieving this state and often feel that meditation is like a light switch — it is either off or on — and that until you achieve this goal of complete stillness, no benefit will flow.

Now the good news: there is a dimmer switch! There is a gradient of experiences and benefits to be gained from meditation. Meditation encompasses a range of experiences, with differing degrees of difficulty and differing effects for us to experience.

We have already discussed the three main pathways of Health, Insight and Creative Meditation. In more general terms, we have described meditation as an altered state of consciousness. In formulating an overall concept of meditation, this is a helpful starting point, for we know that there are a number of different levels of consciousness. By understanding these levels, we can understand more of the intentions and methods of meditation.

Levels of consciousness

Firstly, there is deep sleep, in which we have no conscious awareness. Then, secondly, there is dreaming, where still we are asleep but now we are experiencing something — our dreams. A third state of consciousness is that state of reverie, halfway between sleep and normal wakefulness, which feels quite different to anything else. Then there is our normal waking state, the level of consciousness we are probably most familiar with.

Meditation is yet another state of conscious awareness. Clearly, meditation begins when ordinary day-to-day thinking stops and we enter into another level of what is generally termed higher consciousness.

Before we examine what it is like to experience these higher states of consciousness, and so that we can understand their importance, it is worthwhile spending some time on explaining a little of how our body works and the role of stress in producing disease.

The Fight-or-Flight Response—
a key factor in health and disease

The Fight-or-Flight Response is the well-known instinctive, automatic response our body mounts in reaction to a fearful, challenging situation.

If you suddenly saw a bear lurching in through your doorway, it would be perfectly natural to gasp in fright and to feel a big charge of adrenalin surging through your veins. You would almost surely gulp in a short tight breath of air as the muscles throughout your body tensed. At the same time it would be normal for your heart rate, blood pressure and respiration rate all to increase and for major changes to occur in your hormone levels, the rise in cortisone being particularly significant. Your whole body chemistry would change rapidly, preparing you to react to the challenge. This response is what is known simply as the Fight-or-Flight Response.

Most people know about the Fight-or-Flight Response, but the importance of the sequence that follows it has only recently become more obvious.

In a normal situation, the Fight-or-Flight Response would lead to a period of intense activity — you would attempt to defend yourself against the bear, or you would run away. The changes in body chemistry elicited by the Fight-or-Flight Response are ideal for this purpose; they cover the body's needs during peak exercise and prepare it to deal with any injury you may sustain. This is a very useful self-preservation response, and it occurs instinctively, automatically.

In this sequence, with your body prepared in this manner by the Fight-or-Flight Response, there then follows a fight or a chase — a period of intense physical activity. You get away, you get beaten up, or you win the fight. Then it is over. There is a nice clear end-point. If it is in fact a confrontation with a bear, and you lose, your worries may be over! In most situations, however, the action will come to an obvious end. The emergency is over. Now the cycle needs to be completed. You need to relax again.

The role of relaxation

'Ahhh!' you can say now, letting out a long slow breath and feeling the tension draining from the system, 'It's over!' Your muscles relax. Your heart rate, blood pressure and respiration, in fact your whole body chemistry, settles back to normal maintenance levels.

This essential release of tension is what is described as the Relaxation Response. In a natural, normal situation, we do it effortlessly and effectively.

The importance of all this lies in appreciating that to be relaxed is to be healthy. Now to be relaxed is not to be lethargic, sedentary, slobby. To be relaxed is not necessarily to be lying out under the sun, dozing with a book and a can of beer. It can be that, but it involves a lot more.

To be relaxed is to use the minimal amount of energy required for the task in hand. Not over-exerting; not falling short. Getting the work done with the minimal effort required. If you were lying in the sun and were relaxed, all your muscles would be soft and loose, with no residual unnecessary tension. The same principle, however, applies to running a marathon — use only the amount of effort required, no strain, no over-striving, no tension. A look at the good runners of the world will bear this out. Robert de Castella may be putting in a peak performance in the marathon but he looks basically relaxed. Watch Carl Lewis before a 100-metre sprint; there is no hint of physical tension. There is plenty of loosening up, shaking the legs and arms to release the tension. He knows if his muscles are tight with tension he will have to work against himself to get down the track. Relaxed, he can perform at his peak.

So, to be relaxed is to be efficient, healthy, normal.

To be relaxed is to be healthy.

Stress and the Fight-or-Flight Response

The source of many medical problems nowadays is that the Fight-or-Flight Response is being triggered off by complex life situations which we find difficult to release, difficult to take to a satisfactory conclusion. The Fight-or-Flight Response is being set in motion but its partner, the Relaxation Response, is not.

The reason for this is that the challenges which threaten us in our present-day complex, loose-knit and competitive society are more likely to be of an emotional or mental nature than a physical one. We get the occasional clearcut fright in the traffic and the like, but mostly we are faced with complex situations — dealing with people that irritate us, fears about what might be about to happen, feelings of being locked into insoluble problems.

Every time we go to work for an overbearing boss, or even think about him, the Fight-or-Flight Response is aggravated. Our level of arousal is raised and major changes take place in the balance of our body chemistry. We might feel the tension rising, the urge to hit him or to walk out, but we need the job, the pay, the security, so we swallow hard, contain the feeling, sustain the stress.

Similar effects result from not dealing with an old trauma such as a bereavement — the loss of someone we cared for and still feel unresolved about. Old memories like that can jolt the Fight-or-Flight Response into activity. So can fears for the future: What if I don't get the job? What if I can't pay the bills? What if she doesn't like me? What if the bomb drops? and so on, and on. Tension, tension — and where does it go? Sadly, often enough it goes nowhere, it is not released but builds up and up, creating stress upon stress.

Stress—creative or destructive?

It is helpful to put stress into its proper perspective. Stress can be very useful. If it were not for stress we would never get out of bed in the morning. Whether it be the stress of getting to work on time, the stress of being hungry, or just the stress of needing to go to the toilet, if it were not for stress we would not be motivated to do anything.

The stress curve—a graded response

Like most things, however, a little is positively good for you while a lot creates real problems. The effect of stress on our day-to-day performance is therefore very interesting. No stress, no performance. A little stress, and soon we are feeling good, we have a challenge in our lives, something to do, something to work at, something to achieve.

When we feel on top of a challenge, when it is within our capabilities, even if it is extending us a little, it feels good to be

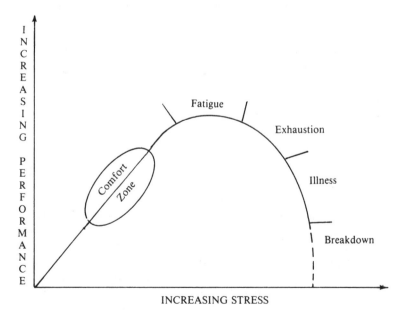

Stress-Performance Graph

meeting that challenge. The stress feels comfortable at this point and its effects are decidedly creative. We are responding well, being motivated and constructive. To be functioning in this way, where we are performing effectively and happily, is well described as being in a Comfortable Zone. This Comfort Zone is the area of our peak performance and efficiency.

As we move to the right of this graph, the challenge in our lives, the stress, is seen to be getting greater. At the same time, the higher the line moves up the graph, the greater the performance we are producing in response to this challenge. So, as we have discussed, a little stress causes a rise in performance and soon we are operating in our Comfort Zone. Here there is enough stress in our life to provide worthwhile, meaningful challenge and we are capable of responding well. Life has zest and meaning.

Extending the Comfort Zone

However, as we can see on the graph, if the pressure becomes a little greater, we may get pushed beyond this Comfort Zone, beyond our ability to cope satisfactorily. We start to become fatigued. Meeting the challenge becomes an effort and our performance begins to taper off. If the stress continues and the pressure keeps building, our performance declines, we start to become exhausted. The warning signals start to sound. Our efficiency falls off, there is reduction in performance. We become more irritable and short-tempered. We might get occasional indigestion or headaches. There is a generalised malaise, we just don't feel right.

If these signals are ignored and we still push on, attempting to meet an ever-increasing stressful challenge, we will soon encounter illness. At first, relatively minor things — skin rashes, irritable bowel, allergies, food sensitivities, even ulcers, and then on into high blood pressure and many other conditions. The American Academy of Physicians claims that at least two-thirds of all visits to general practitioners in America are for primarily stress-related illnesses.

If changes are not made in response to these lesser ailments, major breakdowns can occur. Heart attacks are well known to be precipitated by stress. Over 90 per cent of the thousands of cancer patients I have asked have felt sure that stress was a major contributing factor in the development of their disease.

Take heart, however. The answer is at hand. The Relaxation Response is a reliable and successful way to release that accumulated tension and so it allows a return to normal.

The stress cycle—an integrated summary

Before expanding on the solution, it is very useful to conceptualise this whole process. The following flow chart will help you do this and it is well worth the time to dwell on it. Getting it clear in your mind will help you to understand how stress affects you and why the Relaxation Response is so useful. It also makes sense of why and how the Relaxation Response can and should be learned and practised efficiently and effectively.

Unresolved situations induce stress— creative or destructive?

On the stress cycle chart, the left-hand column represents the mechanics of the Fight-or-Flight Response. Going towards the right we see the impact of being confronted by an unresolved situation. Depending on how we respond to this challenge, this situation, it can be constructive or destructive.

Unresolved situations arise either because we cannot do anything about them or because we try our best but we don't get the result we thought we wanted. Perhaps we are out of work and are trying hard to get a job, but without success. The pressure involved in needing a job is obvious and continuing, but we seem unable to do anything about it. Alternatively, perhaps we do have a job but we are unable to meet our commitments. The overdraft mounts, we try to work harder, but there is no more income. We are doing the best we can, but every time the phone rings we think: Is it the bank manager again? There is a constant feeling of being under pressure to do a little more, to work harder, to make it better for tomorrow.

Acceptance—short circuiting stress

In any such unresolved situation we are faced with a choice. We could say, well, this is the outcome; the conclusion to this challenge is not what I expected or wanted, but I have done my best — that is all I can do, that is the end of it. Be practical, make some adjustments,

The Stress Cycle

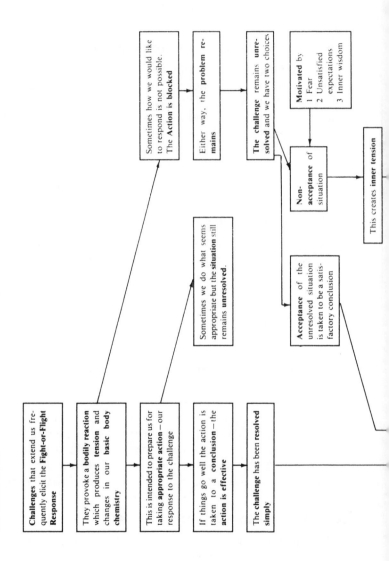

Challenges that extend us frequently elicit the **Fight-or-Flight Response**

They provoke a **bodily reaction** which produces **tension** and changes in our **basic body chemistry**

This is intended to prepare us for taking **appropriate action** — our response to the challenge

If things go well the action is taken to a **conclusion** — the **action is effective**

The **challenge** has been **resolved simply**

Sometimes how we would like to respond is not possible. The **Action is blocked**

Either way, the **problem remains**

Sometimes we do what seems appropriate but the **situation** still remains **unresolved**.

The challenge remains **unresolved** and we have two choices

Acceptance of the unresolved situation is taken to be a satisfactory conclusion

Non-acceptance of situation

Motivated by
1 Fear
2 Unsatisfied expectations
3 Inner wisdom

This creates **inner tension**

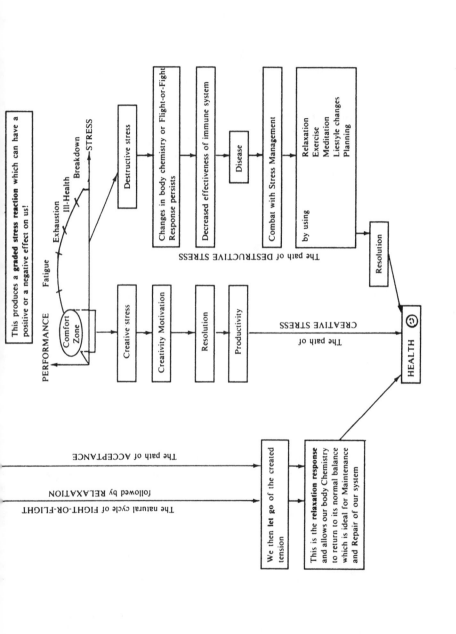

make some changes. Relax and go on to the next thing. No stress. No effort. Life goes on.

I guess if we were all uncomplicated, secure, confident and optimistic beings, that is what we would do. Life being what it is, however, we often seem to get stressed instead.

The causes of stress

There are three things that cause us to not accept a situation: fear, unsatisfied expectations, and Inner Wisdom. Later, we will examine the nature of these three factors in greater detail. Suffice it to say that when any of the three are operating, we are unable to accept the situation. Then we feel we have to do something. This creates an inner tension, we begin to respond to the situation, and stress is provoked.

Creative stress

If we can meet the challenge readily, we experience the Comfort Zone and a positive stress. We enjoy the situation and find ourselves creatively motivated to cope with it. As a result we are likely to take the situation through to a satisfactory conclusion and enjoy peak health along the way.

Destructive stress

If we are pushed beyond our capacity to cope we will experience the situation as a negative stress. Most commonly it is fear that pushes us over the edge, although unsatisfied expectations and, to a lesser extent, Inner Wisdom, can also create an unmanageably negative stressful situation. Either way, if our coping ability is exceeded we will have difficulty raising the required performance to meet the challenge satisfactorily and our health is likely to suffer in the process.

Discharging stress with the Relaxation Response

When stress is a problem, the Relaxation Response is the answer. A very good analogy is seeing the body under stress as being like a battery. As stress builds up, the inner tension is like a charge building up in the battery. When a charged battery is earthed, the current runs out of it; when a stressed person practises the Relaxation Response, that stress is released.

The best thing about this is that the Relaxation Response releases the stress, the tension, regardless of where that stress came from. It does not matter whether a battery was charged by another battery, by mains power electricity, by solar power, by a car, or whatever. If it is earthed, it discharges. The same applies to stress. If stress is present, regardless of how it built up, once you practise the Relaxation Response, the effects of that stress will simply disappear. Nothing else changes immediately, but there is an immediate change in your body chemistry and you will return to a more healthy state of equilibrium.

The effects of using the Relaxation Response

These changes were first defined by Walter Hess in 1957 and have been well-studied since. The physiological changes seen in stressed people who learn to use the Relaxation Response are decreases in muscle tone, heart and respiratory rate, blood pressure, blood lactate and cortisone levels. There is also a noticeable decrease in oxygen consumption and carbon dioxide elimination. Blood flow to the major internal organs increases. Peripheral circulation also improves, causing a rise in skin temperature, and there is an increase in basal skin resistance. In fact, using biofeedback, these last two measures can be used to provide an accurate measure of the extent of the relaxation.

In addition, noticeable changes occur in the brain's electrical patterns—the brain waves. Using an electroencephalogram (EEG), Maxwell Cade has done excellent work in identifying the EEG patterns associated with the different levels of consciousness. This is most helpful in identifying that something measurable does take place during meditation, and it correlates well with meditators' actual experiences. During the Relaxation Response the EEG shows an increase in the intensity of slow alpha waves and occasional theta wave activity. (See Appendix II.)

All these changes indicate that we are talking about a state which is quite different from sleep or ordinary relaxation. It is another state of consciousness accompanied by a state of physiological rest that is much deeper than simple sleep.

Stages of Meditation

Stage of Meditation	Description	State of awareness—experience recorded	Body sensations
1	RELAXATION PHASE (This is not the Relaxation Response. It is a time for concentration on the method of physical relaxation—a transient stage leading from normal consciousness into a more relaxed mental state.)	Most people start by feeling self-conscious, particularly when first learning. They wonder if anything will happen, hope no one is looking. It is common to be conscious of mental activity (many thoughts usually) and to feel some frustration, especially if a beginner.	Feeling the body relaxing. Frequently you become aware of areas of physical tension and feel that tension relaxing.
2	PATCHY CONCENTRATION The concentration is patchy—sometimes good, sometimes wandering off onto other things.	You are conscious of concentrating on the meditation technique. There is a constant stream of thoughts that often you get caught up in. (This is like watching a TV movie when you get so absorbed in the action you forget you are at home watching, you feel like you are in the movie.) Then regularly you come back to an awareness that you are thinking and want it to stop. If not careful, you can get frustrated. Highly subject to being distracted by diversions like inner thoughts or external sounds/activities.	Feel physically relaxed—often this is described as feeling heavy and warm, soft and loose. Actual degree of physical relaxation will increase with time and practice.
3	SUSTAINED CONCENTRATION Single-minded concentration—now the attention is held on one subject. The thinking is still of an intellectual, analytical type.	The mind is becoming stiller and more focussed and there are just occasional unrelated thoughts passing by that do not disturb this basically calm, relaxed state. The intruding thoughts may be current ones or memories and may sometimes produce an emotional response. Fairly regularly there is a conscious awareness of observing these thoughts now and seeing them in a more stable perspective. Often still feel aware of needing to use a technique to maintain this stage.	Body often feels like it is light and there may be sensations of floating. Very occasionally body movements like swaying occur. Usually described as a very pleasant sensation.
4	CONTEMPLATION Single-minded concentration again, but now the thinking is of a more abstract, intuitive type.	Gaps between awareness of thoughts widen, and you experience moments of stillness. Usually you have lost awareness of using a technique. Sense the value of the stillness, find it very satisfying and want to enter into it more deeply—often find it elusive. Often gain minor insights and have creative ideas.	Often described as "funny feeling". The body seems light and as if it is expanding beyond its normal boundaries. Often strange at first, then described as extremely pleasant.

5	TRANSITION A definite stage, bordering between Stages 4 and 6. Most people are aware when they are in this stage, and it requires skill to pass through.	Feel like something is happening, like entering a new level of consciousness. Often described as being on the brink of something extraordinary—both empty and full at the same time. About 25% experience vivid fields of colour, 5% sounds, 5% visions. Often try to record the experience with their intellect and this mind activity prompts a return to level 4. Here people often consciously need to let go and launch into 6, which takes confidence.	The feeling in the head is often described as like having an anaesthetic, or a state of reverie. Body feels light, expansive. Usually feels much bigger than normal—like blown up with a pump—and is furry around the edges. Very pleasant once accustomed to it.
6	UNIFICATION	This is a new level of consciousness marked by an absence of everyday thought and a powerful sense of unity. There are several grades of experience: A *Poor recall*. Not sure if asleep or not but it feels different to sleep. People who have this experience regularly usually note major changes in their health and wellbeing. B *Heightened alertness*. A mystical experience that is difficult to describe to another. Comes with a sense of being an important part of something much bigger than yourself. C *Being conscious of old memories surfacing* from past. Being able to view them like a dispassionate observer and release them. After-effect is not to erase the memory but to take the intensity out of any pain that may have gone with it. (C can occur to a less effective extent in Stage 3 especially; occasionally in Stage 4)	No awareness of body or surrounding environment. An experience beyond the physical body, space and time—like death might be, and because this experience is recorded, it frequently removes all fear of death.
7	ILLUMINATION	Direct perception of Knowledge. New information comes to your awareness with the authority of a revelation. Produces a very assured, satisfied state of inner knowing. Invariably has a quality of a gift from a higher power, and again, produces a pervading sense of order and unity.	As for Stage 6

Associated with these directly measurable changes, comes a return to normal functioning of the immune system. The inner healer is reactivated. This is why practising the Relaxation Response is effective in dealing with such a wide range of disease states.

The Relaxation Response—Meditation's first healthy step

This talk of the Fight-or-Flight Response and the Relaxation Response should help to demystify elements of meditation and to explain why Health Meditation generally has gained so much popularity as a self-help technique. In centuries gone by, meditation was used primarily as a pathway to higher consciousness. It was a long and often arduous path, well suited for those serious about spiritual development. In the practice of Zen, for instance, twenty years was considered a reasonable time to devote to attaining progress. Traditionally, the emphasis was on spiritual gain, and good health was seen merely as a happy by-product.

Western intellect has been useful here. We can now assess the myriads of different styles of meditation and decipher the common, health-promoting factors, the active ingredients that produce immediate results. With our understanding of the physiology of stress and relaxation, we can understand the health benefits of the Relaxation Response. Also, we can readily identify how to elicit the Relaxation Response and how, if we so choose, to aim for higher states of consciousness.

The stages of Meditation

So, if the Relaxation Response is the first step into Health Meditation, what is it like and what of these other higher states?

Based on the testimonies of many people, there is a common range of experience. Some people pass through all these stages of experience, while some circumvent one or more. Some spend most of the time at one level. Most people, however, experience a range of levels on most of the occasions that they sit down to meditate.

What follows is a description of seven stages of meditation. The experiences recorded in each stage, both physically and mentally, are included to provide an idea of what this normal range of experience is like.

Some people pass through these stages so quickly that they are aware of only some of them. The Relaxation Response is characterised by stages 3 and 4, especially 4. Stage 5 is a transient stage and is the last opportunity for our normal intellect to be in the act, for us to have an awareness involving something like our normal conscious experience. Stages 6 and 7 are states of higher consciousness, mystical states that are almost always interpreted by those who enter them as direct personal experiences of a spiritual reality. Again, because these experiences transcend space and time, they frequently free people from mundane fears and produce a feeling of deep contentment.

The benefits of these states

To derive the benefits offered by the Relaxation Response, it has to be practised regularly. If not, the old stress, tension and anxiety patterns will resurface. With practice comes an increased clarity of perception and thinking, increased creativity and efficiency and, as already explained, the rapid reversal of psychosomatic diseases.

Most people who experience the mystical states are powerfully affected by them. They usually talk of having an insight into what is real—what 'is'. They usually develop the concept that there is a fundamental truth and that it can be experienced and known directly. This usually produces a powerful, personal sense of what is right and wrong and a conviction that they can get it right. There is often talk of discovering that there is an inner self, that it is real and trustworthy. This inner self is usually described as being more important, more permanent, more worthwhile than our personality, made up as it is of our body, emotions and rational mind. There is a sense that the personality is an outer, impermanent form and that this inner self is more enduring. Being in contact with this inner self leads to development of Inner Wisdom and a conviction that we do have the potential to discriminate and make good choices in our lives. This is often accompanied by major insight into the meaning of life and what is appropriate for us to do in it.

The mystical states seem to have a great beneficial effect on people's health. Most of the cancer patients I know who have recorded remarkable recoveries would have some experience of them. This experience invariably leads to a positive life orientation, a feeling of order in an otherwise difficult situation, and a conviction that harmony can be sought and found. Meditation is not the only way to find such inner peace, but it is a predictable and reliable way.

The experiences recorded and insights gained through meditation seem almost the same from a wide cross-section of the community. People from a wide range of socio-economic and religious backgrounds seem to reach these same, intensely personally satisfying and pro-life conclusions.

Finally, people who meditate a lot tend to smile a lot! There is often a detectable twinkle in the eye and a quiet smile that comes from deep inside.

The Journey of a Thousand Miles

There is an old Chinese saying that a journey of a thousand miles begins with just one step. Having gained some understanding now of why meditation works and what happens during it, let's get practical again. How do we learn to meditate?

Chapter Three

GETTING STARTED

In order to become satisfied with your meditation and to experience its many benefits, the most important requirement by far is to practise.

There are many practical hints and recommendations that will help you to establish a regular and effective pattern of meditation regardless of what type you are practising. These can be viewed as basic prerequisites but, of course, feel free to seek out what works for you. Happily, meditation is very versatile. Happily also, we are all unique individuals and so we may well have different requirements and find that different things work for us.

Be aware of the need to stay within your meditational Comfort Zone. This is the area which allows you to be learning and practising effectively, enjoying yourself, and perhaps extending yourself a little so that you are developing and fine-tuning your skills. As you learn and practise more, what you need and what will be effective is bound to change.

Based on a wide range of experience, it is possible to highlight the things that consistently have helped others into a good experience with meditation. Your task is to take from these suggestions what you need, what you feel comfortable with, to practise with them and, by so doing, combine them into a technique that works for you.

Clarify your motive

Clarifying your motive for beginning meditation in the first place, and then for doing each session, will set the tone for your whole practice. Being clear on your purpose will also help you to decide upon the practical details, such as the type of meditation to practise and how often to do it.

So, ask yourself question number one: Why are you meditating?

As stated earlier, most people are seeking stress management, relief from an illness and/or personal or spiritual development. Frequently the motive for learning to meditate is based upon fear. There is a concern for the consequences of continuing stress, or fear about the outcome of an illness.

Fear is a powerful motivator. Many people take up meditation thinking to use it to overcome a specific hurdle. Soon, however, their practice becomes satisfying and meaningful. Commonly, the initial motivation of fear is then replaced by a desire to continue the practice for its own sake. Again, being clear on what your intentions are helps greatly. When you have a clear goal, you can set yourself to pursue it and are far more likely to achieve it.

Given even the best of intentions, however, it can still be a challenge to establish a regular meditation routine. Perhaps the biggest limitation to meditation is that you have to do it! The problem is that when you are under stress, when you are busy and feeling overwhelmed, that is the time you most need to meditate. And that is the time when you are inclined to say, 'I'm too busy right now, I'll do it tomorrow.' Tomorrow never comes! Once you miss a few weeks or months of 'tomorrows' it is just that much harder to get re-started.

The practical side of this rests in the fact that there are two important elements to consider — your overall motive in meditating, and your specific motive for each session. Why are you meditating? Stress management, health issues, personal development? Should you concentrate then on Health, Insight, or Creative Meditation, or a combination? Don't procrastinate. Make a decision. My feeling is that everyone should start with the simple, uncomplicated yet powerfully effective Health Meditation and then add to this if and as they need to.

With each session, then, as you settle into your position and begin, take a moment to remind yourself what you are there for. It may simply be to remind yourself that this is a time for Health Meditation. The purpose then is to remove your thoughts from day-to-day, mundane things, to relax physically and allow your mind to be still — all easily, naturally, effortlessly. I like to summarise all this into a little affirmation which encapsulates these ideas. So I say before such sessions:

> *Let your eyes close gently,*
> *Turn your thoughts inwards,*
> *And remember that this is a time for healing.*

The idea is to bring clearly to mind the purpose of the session, whether it be to be mentally still or to focus on a particular technique or creative effort.

Having your motive clear in your mind is essential, but there are also many other things you can do to sustain your practice.

Using positive thinking

The process of getting to the point of actually sitting down, making the time to meditate, and then persuading the mind to stick with the task in hand, can be greatly aided by using well-directed, positive thinking techniques, a subject covered in depth in *You Can Conquer Cancer* (1984).

The mind is a goal-orientated, problem-solving tool. From the myriads of choices that face us every moment, the mind picks the one most likely to meet our needs; those needs being defined by the goals we have set ourselves.

So we are reading this book right now rather than watching TV or playing golf, because our mind has decided this is the best thing for the moment. When our mind is working well for us, making good choices and helping us to achieve them, it actually uses three basic principles. To provide the best chance of success, we can choose to consciously use these three essential principles of positive thinking:

A The three principles of Positive Thinking

1 Have a clearly defined goal.
2 Be prepared to do whatever it takes to achieve that goal.
3 Be prepared to enjoy doing it!

In practical terms, we can break these principles down into a number of steps. Again, when we are working easily and well towards achieving a goal, we do these things effortlessly and naturally. If, however, you are having problems doing what you think you should be doing — for example practising meditation regularly — then check through this list and see what is missing. Each step follows naturally on the others, and if one is missing the whole lot falls.

The steps that make Positive Thinking work

(1)   *Clarity*

The essential starting point, the First Principle of Positive Thinking, is setting a clear goal to aim for. Being clear on why you are learning is a great help in ensuring a good motive. Use reading, talking, listening, thinking, contemplating. Sort through the options and set yourself a specific target. Then, to begin meditation, you need to clarify practical issues like which technique you will use and how often you will practise.

(2)   *Acceptance*

Accept the goal. Accept that, given your present condition and what you currently are aware of, this is the best decision you can make. So accept that it is good and necessary to give time to your meditation. Do not allow yourself to get immersed in thoughts like, 'I should be doing the vacuuming or finishing that report'. Be clear that by doing your meditation your whole efficiency will rise, you will feel better and be more effective. This is time that you need to give to yourself.

(3)   *Commitment*

Determine then to commit yourself to your accepted goal. Successful people are remarkable for their high level of commitment. As the Second Principle says, be prepared to do whatever it takes. Make the time, go to classes, practise and follow through.

(4)   *Discipline*

Make sure you carry through. If you have clearly established the three previous steps, your motivation will be high and the discipline will follow easily. Take it as a warning of personal danger if you find yourself consistently not living up to your goals, and in this situation seek personal counselling. Attending a group adds an outside discipline and regularity, as does meditating regularly with your partner.

(5)   *Perseverance*

Be prepared for natural cycles of ups and downs and for occasional set backs. Successful people display the ability to 'bounce back'. In meditation, regularity of practice is the most important factor of all.

(6) *Reinforcement*

Seek out ways of reinforcing your intentions. Join with friends or a group to meditate, listen to tapes, read other books, keep quiet with those who oppose you and seek out the company of those who value what you are doing.

(7) *Reassessment of your progress*

Is your practice improving things? Are you getting closer to your goals? If not, why not? What can you do to improve things?

(8) *Enjoy!*

Above all, enjoy what you are doing. If you are not enjoying yourself, at least one of the above is either missing or incomplete. Check and see — are you clear about why you have set this goal, and are you following through on it? If you are doing both of these things, it should be a real pleasure.

Choosing your method

The whole book is intended to clarify this basic question for you. Chapters 3, 4 and 5 specifically address this area.

The standard recommendation is that everyone is likely to benefit from Health Meditation. Most find the Progressive Muscle Relaxation as described in Chapter 4 a good place to begin. Remember that the simpler the technique the better, so seek out the simplest method that works for you. Once you have developed some skill with Health Meditation, if you want to, try some Insight or Creative Meditation.

When you begin using a new technique, it is wise to practise it for several weeks. This gives you time to get to know it and to be able to do it without having to think about it, that is, to develop some flowing skill with the method. After a few weeks you will know if the technique is working for you, and whether you need to adapt it, discard it, or continue more or less intensively.

The benchmark is, does the technique leave you feeling better than before? Are you frustrated, or are you feeling satisfied? Frequently you will need to persevere when things are not going well, when they do not seem as you had hoped for—that is normal and natural. So, if you are content to be persevering with a technique and you can see that you are in a learning phase, then each session is an investment in getting better, progress is being made, and you are wise to continue. If you find yourself getting anxious or frustrated, however, seek further help through another technique or a teacher.

Teachers and Groups

Neither are essential. Both are helpful.

Particularly for Health Meditation, you can do it yourself if you are committed. A teacher or group that you have regular contact with is likely to smooth out the ups and downs and speed the learning process, but you can do it on your own. If you are going it alone, books and tapes are an invaluable aid.

For Insight Meditation, a teacher can be of more use in directing your progress, but again this is not absolutely essential. There clearly are some pitfalls to watch out for with these techniques, but most people find that when their need for a teacher is real, they are magnetically drawn to the correct person.

Recommendations for the practice of Meditation

1   Time requirements

(a)   *In the beginning*

When you are beginning, particularly if you are concentrating on Health Meditation, it is wise to consider doing three sessions daily until you get into a routine and feel that your meditation is taking effect. This is because each formal session will produce a residual beneficial period. At first, you may feel a benefit for only ten or thirty minutes after a session. If you do another session fairly soon after the first, this 'positive hangover' effect will extend and soon it will link up with the next meditation period. With practice you will find each session adding to the next and soon you will have a positive snowball building your health and well-being.

Also, when you are beginning, do not exceed what seems comfortable for you. You may think twenty minutes is what you need. For ten minutes you may feel happy sitting there and then get restless. Keep sitting as long as you do not get frustrated. If you are content to be there, seeing the extra time as practice, an investment in learning to do it better, then by all means persevere. If, however, you feel that you are about to explode, it is better to get up and return again later. There is no need to turn a stress management technique into a stressful event! Begin where you can be comfortable, being confident that as you practise you will be able to sit comfortably for longer periods.

(b) *How long?*

Ten to twenty minutes twice a day seems to provide the benefits the Relaxation Response has to offer. This short time spent practising this basic form of Health Meditation can produce all the health benefits meditation has to offer. So, for stress management and basic health requirements, the time commitment is best considered to be around twenty minutes twice a day.

When using Health Meditation in managing a major illness, it appears that there is an increasing return for increasing practice, up to about three sessions daily of one hour each. This amount of time seems to provide maximum benefit in terms of stimulating inner healing. People have certainly done more than this but the feeling is, if you want the maximum benefit, that this is a good goal to aim for. Please appreciate that these recommendations are based purely on the direct experience of people like the late Dr Ainslie Meares and myself. So far as I am aware, there have been no specific trials to measure the impact of varying the time spent on meditation.

For Insight Meditation, the longer periods are generally more satisfactory — usually one half to a full hour at each session. You will need to experiment to find your own best level here.

Creative Meditation can take a variable time, but often short, frequent periods are ideal.

Summarising, a practical minimum would seem to be one session of ten to twenty minutes daily; an upper range, one hour three times daily. If even ten minutes seems too long for you, start where you can and build up. If you do have trouble being physically still for ten minutes, I would strongly recommend joining a group, and also, almost certainly, you would find massage a great help.

It is highly recommended to aim for a minimum of at least one meditation session each day.

(c)   *Short or long?*

The question often arises, is one long session better or worse than two shorter sessions? In general, the answer is that, for Health Meditation, two sessions are desirable. For Insight Meditation, longer sessions are useful — so, here then, if your time is limited, one longer session may well be preferable. Creative Meditation is often best done in short, regular sessions.

Most meditators find, once they have established a basic routine of ten to twenty minutes twice daily, that they become sensitive to their own needs and can satisfactorily gauge whether they need to do more or less.

(d)   *Time of day*

Traditionally the ideal periods were said to be at sunrise and sunset. In practice you can make your own choices. For preference it is better to meditate before a meal rather than after, but again this is not essential.

First thing in the morning is an excellent time — if you are reasonably awake! It has been a triumph of positive thinking (and twelve years in the making) that has recently seen me getting up early to meditate! If you can do so, the house and atmosphere are generally quiet and conducive to meditation.

Meditating in the evening affects people differently. Traditionally it was recommended not to meditate regularly after dark. In practice, some find that they fall off to sleep too easily; others find it so invigorating that they do not sleep. Still others find it successful. You will have to review your daily priorities and experiment. As an ideal I would recommend early in the morning after a shower and possibly a few exercises, followed by a second session before the evening meal. If you are doing a third session it would fit in well before you have lunch.

(e)   *Regularity*

Being able to meditate at the same time each day is a distinct advantage. Having a routine makes getting it done far more reliable. It is then less likely to be put off until a bit later, which becomes 'I'll do it tomorrow'.

A routine also takes away any anxiety of 'When can I fit it in today?' If you can link up your meditation practice with other established routines, such as after the morning shower or before meals, it makes it particularly easy to integrate it into your daily life.

My guess is that once you practise you will feel meditation has an important, ongoing place in your life. If you want to establish it as such, it will need to become a daily habit like having a shower or eating three meals each day.

Meditating at the same time each day, then, while not essential, is a great advantage.

(f) *Timing*

When is the time up? How will I know when to stop? These common questions are easily answered.

Most practically, use an alarm clock or a kitchen timer. If you do so, make sure the noise of the alarm is soft or that you muffle it, to avoid undue shock when it goes off. Having it in an adjoining room, in a cupboard, or under a pillow should be quite effective. Alternatively, ask someone to knock or just quietly to tell you when your allotted time is up. You could also use a tape that has an introduction, then a period of silence, followed by words to finish with. My meditation practice tapes are on C90s which provide 45 minutes of meditation each side.

An interesting and exciting revelation for most new meditators is their ability to set their own inner alarm clock. Most people are pleasantly surprised how accurate this system is. If you have ten minutes, sit down and tell yourself that you will finish in ten minutes. If you have an hour, set yourself for the hour. Most people find with a little practice that their inner clock is reliable to within a minute or two.

(g) *Visitors, phones, and other intruders!*

It is highly desirable to decide at the outset how you will handle the front doorbell ringing, the telephone, and visitors that stay into your meditation time.

Again, a clear understanding of priorities is an asset. Is your meditation essential, or is it a luxury? Are you casual, or serious?

Another hazard comes from the animal kingdom. Animals, especially cats, love to be around or, preferably, on people who are meditating! If you can handle your cat purring and kneading your lap while you are being still, that's fine. Most decide that the animals need to watch from afar.

Here are some people's creative solutions to common intrusions:

— A notice on the front door: 'Do not disturb — In an altered state'.
— Simply not responding to the doorbell or telephone, being confident that if it was important they will call again.
— Ensuring your partner can take messages.
— If you meditate together you may choose to take it in turns to do the answering.
— Being prepared to get up to answer the telephone, to not become annoyed, and return to meditation, aiming to hold the feeling of the meditation as you do so.
— For a patient beset by too many visitors, telling your visitors, 'Look, you know how sick I have been recently and I really don't want to die. The meditation is really helping me and I would like to do it in ten minutes' time. Please come in and stay for a short while.' This technique is guaranteed to have your house clear in around seven minutes — eight at the most!

Obviously, there is a need to assert yourself, to establish your needs, gently but effectively. Do whatever it takes to get it done.

Location

Meditating in the same place each day is another helpful device. That place will start to take on an association with meditation. Just as you expect to go to sleep when you go to bed, so you will expect to meditate when you go to this place.

Some people have the luxury of a spare room they can keep solely for meditation. Most find that there is at least a corner of a room that can be put aside. It can be very helpful to have a chair, or a cushion or mat, whatever you are using, that is kept exclusively for when you meditate.

You may also like to decorate the area and make it more tranquil, more sympathetic to your intentions. A meaningful photograph, or a painting of peaceful scenery, can add to the atmosphere. You may prefer a spiritual theme with a picture, a statue, or a cross. Many people enjoy placing fresh flowers in their meditation area. Lighting a candle before you begin can add a sense of reverence and 'specialness' to each occasion.

In fact, having a small 'ritual' of setting flowers, lighting a candle and pondering your picture can help you make the transition from the day-to-day mundane things, towards the state of inner stillness. This 'ritual' can have a definite religious air to it if that is your choice, or it can have a more abstract flavour. Recognise that this is a special time for you, a time to get to know yourself better, to build your self-respect and draw on your own inner talents.

Some people like some exercise before their meditation. Yoga and/or breathing exercises are particularly suitable. So, too, are bending and stretching exercises, and walking. Some find that even more strenuous exercise suits them. Others find reading, particularly on a subject relevant to meditation or on a spiritual theme, can be a good way to settle a little before beginning a session. Again, these things are not essential, but they can be helpful.

When you begin learning to meditate, it is a definite advantage to feel secure and to be in a relatively quiet area. In the beginning it can be quite disconcerting if you have to worry over who is going to see you sitting there with your eyes shut. The middle of a busy office is not the place to begin. Find a quiet place, away from the bustle, where you can be confident of remaining uninterrupted.

At home, make the best arrangements you can with the other family members. It is generally unreasonable and unnecessary to expect the rest of the household to come to a standstill while you do! However, it is nice if they will turn down the stereo and avoid sudden loud noises. As you practise, these outside distractions will become less of an issue. To begin with, it is helpful to minimise them.

Progress to more challenging situations

Do bear in mind that you do not want to get hooked on absolutely having to meditate in a particular place at a particular time. We are talking here of ways of creating an ideal environment that will support you in your early endeavours. As you progress, you may well choose to do the bulk of your meditation in your favourite, special spot. But, please, do be adventurous. Occasionally, at least, go to another place, sit in another chair, choose a noiser background. This will all help you to retain or develop some flexibility.

Using more challenging environments from time to time will help you to become able to retain the meditation quality during your day-to-day activities and it will also help you into a deeper experience of meditation. Curiously, the more challenging or difficult your starting point, the more likely it is that if your meditation is working you will go deeper. This is because you have to concentrate more clearly and selectively to overcome the increased distractions and so you tend to go deeper. This presumes you do not exceed your Comfort Zone, what you can cope with, for if you do you will probably get nowhere.

Experiment. Find out what you like and what is effective — for you.

Position

There are two basic requirements for a satisfactory meditation position:

1   *Symmetry*

When your position is symmetrical it gives a feeling of physical balance. This leads to a feeling of internal balance which is what we are after. It also provides a formal, special air to it all. Meditation is not some lackadaisical business where we flop down any old how. This is something special, something important, and the position should reflect this. A gentle, balanced discipline is required.

2   *A little discomfort*

An element of discomfort is your best insurance against going to sleep. Tuck snugly into bed and try to meditate, and you will almost certainly lapse into sleep. As you practise more and get used to it, you will probably be able to remain awake and meditate wherever you are, but beds are associated with sleep and meditation is best done elsewhere if possible.

Traditional positions are a trifle intimidating for most modern Westerners. For some beginners, sitting in the lotus position, your legs crossed and your feet up on opposite thighs, is likely to be an invitation to agony rather than stillness.

Happily, you do not need to tie yourself in knots in order to be effective. The position should be relatively easy for you, just a mild sense of discomfort, especially for Health Meditation.

There is a range of positions to consider. Ranking them in ascending order of difficulty will allow you to try a few and discover what is best to begin with. The positions are demonstrated by Gayle in the accompanying photographs in this chapter.

Choosing a position

1 *Lying* (See fig. 1.)

For most people, lying is the most comfortable position. If you use it, lying on a hard surface is best. Again, most beds are too comfortable for effective meditation. A floor covered with a blanket to shield out the cold is ideal, or you may prefer to use a thin mat.

Lie flat on your back, legs out straight and a little apart. Let your feet flop comfortably outwards but, if this strains any ligaments, support them vertically by placing pillows beside them. Let your arms lie naturally, basically straight, and a little out from your sides. It is best to have your hands open, palms up, fingers gently extended, free of tension. You should be looking up to the ceiling or sky, with your chin slightly towards the chest. Do not let your head fall to one side. You may prefer to place a small pillow or cushion under your head, but keep it as flat as possible. Some people find raising their knees with a cushion is an advantage.

A lounge can be good to lie on. The outdoor furniture type can be adjusted to lift the upper body and this may suit some people with special needs.

2 *Sitting*

(a) *In an armchair*

The most comfortable is a lounge chair with a high back. Sit squarely, feet on the floor, a little apart. I recommend that you sit up straight as this is more balanced and places less strain on the back. The body should be upright and the arms can rest comfortably on the chair's arms. Here the palms are best placed downwards over the ends of the chair. The head should stay erect although it could well rest back against the chair if it is high enough. Ideally, the chin should be tucked in a little towards the chest so that the head is poised in balance and the neck is free of any tension.

(b) *In an armless chair* (See figs. 3 and 4.)

This is one of the most satisfactory positions for beginners. In our groups we use square-backed stackable chairs with a padded base and back. These provide support for a good, symmetrical position and are just comfortable enough to allow most people to be able

Positions for Meditation

Fig. 1 Lying

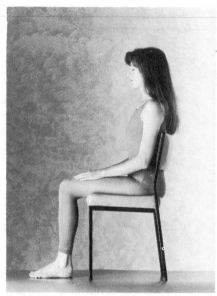

Fig. 2 In an armless chair (1)

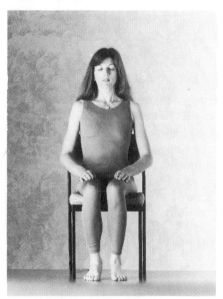

Fig. 3 In an armless chair (2)

Fig. 4 On an ergometric chair

Fig. 5 Sitting with legs crossed

Fig. 6 Traditional Yoga Lotus position

Fig. 7 Zen meditation pose

Fig. 8 Candle gazing

to use them for quite long sessions. We encourage people to sit in them with their backs vertical, initially resting against the back support. As they progress, we recommend at least trying some sessions sitting forward without this support.

The back should be vertical. A good mental picture is achieved by thinking of the spine and head as being balanced like a pile of coins. Once you gain this sense of balance, it takes very little effort to maintain this vertical position. The head should be maintained erect, chin down a little.

It is preferable to make right angles of the angles made by the body and thighs at the hips, the thighs and calves at the knees, and the calves and feet at the ankles. For long people, this may mean raising the chair a little higher by putting it on a board or two. For short people, there may be a need to place boards or a cushion under the feet so that they make a comfortable contact.

The hands should rest comfortably on the thighs, usually palms down with fingers gently outstretched. Some prefer to turn their palms up or cup them in their laps, but the former feels very balanced and comfortable.

(c) *Other chair types* (See fig. 2.)

Some people have found stools useful, while more recently the newer, ergometric type of kneeling chair such as the 'Balans' have proven very satisfactory and popular. They tilt the pelvis and provide a very stable, sensible position. A simpler version can be made from a piece of wood used as a sloping support, itself held up by two side pieces.

(d) *Traditional postures*

Out of the long tradition of Eastern meditation have come two quite similar meditation postures. Both based on the lotus position, they vary in their hand positions. Firstly, one sits on the floor, back and head erect, feet crossed. Then one leg is lifted up on to the opposite knee, the second crossed over on to its opposite knee. This is the basis of the lotus position.

The traditional Hindu or Yoga position then involves the arms being held out straight with the hands resting on the knees. The fingers are first held out straight, then just the forefinger is curled around so that its tip touches the tip of the thumb. (See fig. 6.)

A more traditionally Zen Buddhist posture involves the hands being cupped in the lap, one on top of the other. The fingers are kept straight and close by each other. As you look down, the second knuckle of the middle finger of each hand should overlap. The tips of the thumbs should be touching comfortably. The arms should hang loosely, a little out from the sides. (See fig. 7.)

Sitting on the floor in this manner can be done directly on the floor or, preferably in my opinion, with a cushion under your backside. In Zen, a traditional cushion called a Zafu is used for this purpose. It raises your back, tilts the pelvis and produces a very stable position which can be maintained for a long time.

(e) *Some other sitting postures*

Other sitting positions that can be used on the floor are the half lotus where just one leg is placed up on its opposite thigh. This is a way to practise and loosen up before embarking on the full lotus. More simply, you can just sit with legs crossed. (See fig. 5.) A position that women particularly often find comfortable and suitable is sitting on folded legs with the hands resting on the knees. (See fig. 8 in conjunction with the Candle gazing method of Meditation.)

3 *Moving Meditations*

There are several traditional meditation techniques that are based on movement. Each of these has a quite intricate series of movements and would need to be studied with a good teacher. So Yoga, Tai Chi, and the whirling dancing of the Sufi dervishes, are all the basis for meditation. The quality of these types of meditation is quite different to the static meditations. They take quite a while to learn and to become effective, but are well suited to some people.

A more readily approachable moving meditation is the walking meditation of Zen named Kin Hin. In this practice, one walks slowly, taking one step with each breath. One progresses only the length of the foot with each step. The hands are folded in front just below the ribs.

The ideal position

What you need is a symmetrical position that is just a little uncomfortable. If you are used to exercise and are fairly flexible, you may be well suited to squatting on the floor. For most people, however, the basic chair is ideal. If you have back problems, or difficulty sitting for a longer period, lying down may be the answer.

Experiment and find what suits you best. You may well find that different positions lead you to different qualities of meditation. For instance, for me, if I have been working hard in the garden and I am tired, I will lie down and enjoy relaxing deeply. Usually, however, I find I experience a better quality of meditation if I sit cross-legged on the floor. Mind you, it took me a long time to be able to maintain this position for a long period of time. Most of the early meditation I did when I was ill was done lying on my back. You, too, may find that different positions are appropriate to different times in your routine and your life.

Attitude

Taking the right attitude into meditation is an essential factor in establishing a satisfying practice regime.

The challenge is that most of us these days have been brought up with the concept that the more effort we put into something, the bigger the return. So, if we are keen to meditate, and value it highly for its potential benefits, there is a natural inclination to try hard to do it well, to make it happen, to get it right. Unfortunately, this is not what is needed!

In meditation we are seeking to experience another state of consciousness, a state different from normal day-to-day, rational, intellectual thinking. If we are using that intellect to try and make meditation 'happen', then obviously the intellect is still active and we are stuck where we started. What we are seeking is to transcend the intellect and to experience another part of our mind's activity. The intellect needs to take a holiday – to have some time out.

How can we do this? How can we set about doing something important without trying to make it happen? It sounds like a conundrum! The answer is that the attitude we begin with is of fundamental importance.

Firstly, we do not want to just blank out. This is not sleep we are aiming for, nor is it just a mindless reverie. This is the mystery of meditation. Good meditation brings a feeling of being very alert, even when there is no actual thinking going on. This probably sounds strange if you have not experienced it yet — to be alert and yet not thinking of anything. It sounds strange because it is the intellectual part of your mind which is trying to understand rationally what it is like. Of course, your intellect cannot imagine what it is like when it is not around.

There is a comforting similarity, however, in trying to understand rationally a simple thing like the taste of some new exotic fruit. If you were trying to make up your mind whether to eat a guava or not, you could get some idea of what you were in for by reading or discussing it with someone who had already tasted one. You, yourself, would never be sure of its real taste, however, until you took the plunge and actually tried eating one.

So, given that we want to, how do we experience this stillness of the seemingly ever-active mind? Firstly, we must aim not to try and make it happen. Secondly, we must aim not to assess how we are going. Both these activities are functions of the rational, thinking mind and are major barriers to progress.

The right attitude is like the one you would have when going in to see a good, entertaining film. Imagine going to something light and happy. You know you are not going to be scared out of your shoes, it is likely to be enjoyable, and no one is going to quiz you after the show on what happened. You can just go in, sit down and relax, with a positive expectancy that something nice is about to take place.

This positive expectancy is so very useful when beginning meditation. It is useful to have in mind a thought like, 'This is going to be entertaining'. As we discussed at the beginning of this chapter, clarifying your motive is very useful in setting the tone for your practice. So you can say, 'This is a time for healing' with that same sense of gentle, positive expectancy, but then do not dwell on it. Set the tone and let it happen.

The right attitude with which to begin a meditation session, then, is a fairly neutral one, free of a sense of striving and marked by a purposeful but gentle and positive anticipation.

The other aspect of the film analogy is that there is a real benefit in having an attitude of being an impartial observer. Here the idea is that it is desirable to be aware of watching your own thoughts without actually getting caught up in them. The analogy is that when we are watching an exciting action movie, we forget that it is an illusion up there on the screen that we are watching. We become so engrossed that we feel like we are driving the car, chasing the baddie, whatever.

In meditation, we need to remember that we are observing. Observing our mental processes rather than being caught up by them creates a mental state of discriminating alertness. This teaches us how to focus our attention on whatever we choose and to prevent other things from intruding. Again, this quality is what we have already described as mindfulness — the ability of our mind to hold its attention on what it chooses without forgetting it or wandering on to other things. If you are serious about your meditation, it is well worth considering practising some of the specific techniques designed to develop this skill. The most suitable are based on watching the breathing and are described in Chapter Six. These techniques can act as a very suitable prelude or introduction to Health Meditation as it is quite possible to move on from this state of selective concentration, into a state of mental stillness.

So, to summarise, there clearly are things we need to do to meditate well. One is to have this attitude of mindfulness or discriminating alertness. There are techniques that are very useful. Over and above this, however, is the more important thing of *not trying*. It may sound peculiar at first to say that we know what we want to do but we have to try not to do anything! But, when you understand what is involved, this is not a Catch 22 situation. One of the major things we *must* do to meditate well, is *not* to strive, not to try and make it happen. Just doing it is enough! We must also resist the temptation to judge or assess how we are going. We must be content just to do it.

The right attitude, then, is to settle back in a passive, gentle way with a keen interest in seeing what happens. No great expectations, let's just do this thing, practise the technique, let it flow and see what happens. When you can do just that, something will happen!

Getting started—a summary

When beginning, it is worth taking time to create an environment as near to ideal as you can. Do all you can to ensure success. So, clarify your motives, your aims. Work out what technique you will use, where you will do it and when, and what position you will take up. Remember the Comfort Zone concept. Make it easy to begin with, choose a quiet time of day, go to a quiet place and do all you can to help your practice. You may need to experiment a little with all the options we have discussed, so that you can find your own ideal.

Remember that as your skill develops, you will find it an advantage to do some practice in more challenging situations. Use a more uncomfortable position, or go to a location where there are more potential distractions. Using these challenges helps to develop that quality of selective concentration, mindfulness. It teaches you to be able to direct your attention, to enter into meditation despite the distractions. This in turn leads to being able to retain the beneficial qualities of the meditation — the focussed awareness, the calm, the relaxation — during your daily activities.

So start in a conducive environment under as ideal conditions as possible, and then see it as part of the learning process to advance to more challenging situations.

Reinforcement—an ongoing need

The final consideration in this practical area, is to be aware of the need to sustain your practice. Think of your efforts in learning to meditate as being like a young flower that needs to be looked after, protected and nurtured. Seek out ways to reinforce and sustain your good intentions and efforts.

So, seeking out a group is an excellent idea. Whether it be with an experienced teacher or just with a group of like-minded friends, meeting regularly will reinforce your interest. It will provide access to new techniques, provide contact with like minds with whom you can discuss your progress, as well as adding to the discipline you require.

Remember not to talk too much about your experiences with casual people. Meditation is best done — not assessed or analysed too much. If you are having difficulties or good experiences, share them with a teacher or a like mind, but otherwise let the benefits of your meditation speak for themselves, by showing up in your daily life. When people come up to you and say, 'Wow! What have you been doing? You look so well', that is a good time to tell them.

However, if you are undergoing medical treatment and using meditation, then I do recommend you tell your doctors, if they did not start you in the first place. This keeps them informed and allows them to see the benefits, too!

Books are a very useful means of reinforcing your meditation. There is a recommended reading list at the end of this one. Reading will help you develop new skills while it clarifies and strengthens what you are already doing.

Cassette tapes can add another dimension via the spoken word and music. This can provide a closer link with a teacher and help guide you through your practice. Listening to a tape can lead you through the practice so that you have no need to be thinking of what to do next. This can facilitate your moving from intellectual thinking into a stiller state. Tapes, however, do tend to hold the attention to some degree, so that it is hard to become completely still with them on. This applies to spoken or music tapes.

The tapes are most useful in helping to lead you into a more relaxed state than normal, but for full advantage there is a need to progress beyond an awareness of the tape.

So, if you are using a tape, do not use it all the time. You may well find tapes a great help when beginning, but then, as you progress, wean yourself from them and only use them occasionally. If, at a later stage, you go through an unproductive period where distractions seem rampant, tapes may again help lead you back into the stillness.

Using music tapes with meditation can be a very pleasant experience. You may care to do it purely for the enjoyment. As a side effect, it is also very relaxing.

Another very useful means of reinforcing your meditation, and deepening it, is by attending a meditation intensive. We have found that conducting one-day meditation seminars is an excellent way to get into a good experience of meditation, to have a refresher, or just to enjoy the company of a large group of other meditators. The cumulative effect of a large group over a period like this can be very powerful and there are groups around the country organising these sessions.

To round off, it is important not only to get started with learning to meditate, but to keep going. Be aware of the need to take active steps to maintain your practice, for actually doing it is the most important part of meditation.

So, having established an attitude, a place, time and position for meditation, what do we actually do? Let us begin with Health Meditation.

Chapter Four

MEDITATION FOR HEALTH— INTEGRAL MEDITATION

The aim of Health Meditation is to re-establish or maintain our natural state of equilibrium.

While travelling in the Philippines, Gayle and I had the good fortune to be guided by a young boy with great insight. Alan, at fourteen, had wisdom far beyond his years. After a few weeks I asked Alan if he meditated. He looked at me in a puzzled, querying way. It was as if I had asked him as basic a question as did he eat. My next question surprised him still more. I asked how he learned to meditate. Alan laughed and laughed and then his reply provided an insight:

'Where I live', he said, 'everyone meditates but no one learns to meditate'. It turned out that they just did it. It was a natural function. The parents did it, the grandparents did it, and the children grew up with it. They never lost it, never had to do anything to gain it. There was no need to learn.

Regularly each day, these people would just be still. No tricks, no technique—just be still. Physically relaxed, mind still. Easy. Natural. Simple. This is the essence of what we have described as Health Meditation.

But here is the rub. We western people are very conscious of this highly developed thing between the ears called an intellect. When we sit with the intention of being still, relaxing physically is often not too difficult. But persuading the mind to be still—well, that is another matter!

So, for us, Health Meditation is really learning to regain the natural ability to be still.

Young children often do it. Watch them. Sitting quietly, they gaze off into space, quite 'in another world'. Often we chide them, especially teachers in classrooms: 'Snap out of it. Don't daydream. Pay attention.' And so they are trained to keep thinking, to keep their minds active, and to not take time out.

Then later in life, we have to make this effort to re-learn what we once had, the skill and art of simply being still.

People who learn Health Meditation find that, fairly regularly, the feeling re-kindles childhood memories. Recently John K. found that his first experience of meditation brought a flashback. He said the feeling was just like when he was a young child confined in his playpen. His mum was nearby, he felt safe and secure, had all his favourite toys in with him, and he remembered this feeling of deep contentment. Nothing to do, no expectations, just the joy of simply being there.

So, how do we learn to be still? There are several basic options. While describing them we can discuss which one you should begin with.

Option 1—Using no method

The Direct Approach — just do it. Use no technique. Like Alan, our young friend in the Philippines, just sit and be still. This is like taking the helicopter ride straight to the top of the mountain.

Obviously this would be a wonderful, simple ideal — if we could do it. It certainly is an ideal to work towards. All the other methods we shall discuss should be considered as stepping-stones towards this direct approach. The simpler and less complicated your technique, not only the easier will it be, but the more effective.

An ability to use this direct approach can sometimes be developed by beginners who have contact with an experienced teacher or who are part of an effective meditation group. Scientifically, electro-encephalogram (EEG) studies have confirmed that a person who is deeply in meditation can trigger the meditation response in another person. Traditionally, in India, the transference of one person's experience of meditation, leading to the spontaneous experience of meditation in a beginner is called *shaktipat*. It is a basic tenet especially of the Siddha Yoga school, where the guru is known to be capable of conveying this experience.

In a non-spiritual sense, many people who attended sessions

conducted by the late Dr Ainslie Meares noticed the extra depth of meditation they experienced when he or his assistant touched them. The feeling of meditation, the experience, can be conveyed and lead to direct appreciation.

Certainly, people in my groups have experienced this, particularly those who are prepared to let their intellect go into neutral for a period and are content to just experience what happens. They will often go directly and rapidly into a deep and satisfying experience of meditation. At the groups we often move around the people, putting our hands on them. My wife Gayle, and others with whom I work, have this ability to help people into deeper experience.

For some people, then, the path can be direct and easy. Having had this initial experience they find they can remember what it felt like, are assured that there really is nothing that they need to do and all that is required is to let go. To let go and let it happen. I must admit that it always causes me to smile when I see people falling so easily into meditation.

A big hope in writing this book is to help you to satisfy your intellect enough to really appreciate that this type of meditation begins when everything else stops. When we can just do nothing, be alert and be still, we will experience the joys and benefits of deep meditation.

Unfortunately, most of us have active brains. We sit down, close our eyes and become amazed by the constant stream of thought, the inner chatter, the purposeless dialogues, debates and dilemmas that seem to flood our brains with unceasing trivia and distractions. Whew!

For many, then, this direct approach is too simple! To begin with, how do I do nothing?

Often it is actually helpful, and indeed necessary, to learn to develop a technique that enables us to move from being in our normal conscious state to being still.

Option 2—Using a method: Integral Meditation

Once we understand what is required, we can identify the conditions that need to be fulfilled, if in fact we do need to use a method, to enter into the simple state of Health meditation. The basic intention is to relax physically and to still the mind.

Remember the theory:

Beginning with the Relaxation Response
> A gradient of benefit as we move towards a still mind in a still body
> Aiming to find a way to relax physically and to bring the mind to a point of stillness — simply, naturally, effortlessly — alert and quietly powerful
> Stepping stones from the conscious, waking state to peaceful meditation
> No effort, no striving, no assessment
> A method that flows effortlessly
> Skill — doing it with understanding, but without active thinking
> An altered state of consciousness that goes beyond the intellect
> Still body, still mind

The easiest and most reliable technique that leads into Health Meditation is what I describe as INTEGRAL MEDITATION. This technique provides something that has a definite structure and can be practised readily.

Integral Meditation integrates all the necessary requirements for effective and satisfying Health Meditation.

Integral Meditation uses the Relaxation Response as its first step. This enables us to learn how to let go of all tension, physical and mental. Combined with the right attitude and environment, this practice should then flow effortlessly into the stiller realms of meditation.

In other words, Integral Meditation is a particular method of eliciting the Relaxation Response. It is used because it is the method most likely to lead on into the deeper experience of Health Meditation.

To begin the practice of Integral Meditation let us, therefore, begin by studying the Relaxation Response in practical detail.

1 Four steps to the Relaxation Response

To experience and utilise the Relaxation Response we will need to satisfy four basic conditions:

1 *A suitable position*

You will need a position that is symmetrical and slightly

uncomfortable. This should be in an environment that you find conducive to being still and where you can expect to be undisturbed for the required period.

2 *A means of physical relaxation*

Next you need a technique that leads to physical relaxation. This technique is detailed in the next section.

3 *The quality of passive observation*

While doing this you will require a passive approach that avoids trying to make something happen, assessing progress or worrying (these attitudes activate thinking and lead to arousal rather than relaxation). You should aim to be alert and to passively observe what happens, rather than to evaluate it. This attitude was summarised in Chapter Three and is reinforced throughout the book.

4 *A shift in conscious awareness*

Finally, you require a technique that helps to move your level of consciousness from its normal day-to-day activity into a simpler, more abstract way of being. This technique is generally based on a variety of exercises involving concentration. The basic method is covered in this chapter and other options are included in Chapter Five.

2 *Practising the Relaxation Response*

The first step is to still the body.

Step 1—Physical relaxation

There is a very simple and effective way to learn how to relax physically. It is called the Progressive Muscle Relaxation (PMR) Exercise. This is a traditional technique, developed from the ancient Yoga experience with relaxation. It is a rapid and reliable way of releasing tension and letting go physically. It is very straightforward, and most people find they can do it well within the first day or two of practising. It leads directly to the experience and benefits of the Relaxation Response and is an ideal starting point. It is used as the basis for Integral Meditation.

The technique relies on focussing your attention on different muscle groups in the body and learning how to relax them at will. The simple key to this is being able to focus your attention and to feel the level of tension or relaxation in your body.

So, as a first step, how do we focus our attention where we want it?

A   *Focussing your attention*

Where is your centre? If you had to locate the centre of your consciousness, your self, where would it be? Especially when you close your eyes, where are you?

Most people feel that 'they' are in their heads. Some locate their centre in their chest, heart, or in their solar plexus, but for most the centre feels as if it is somewhere towards the front of the forehead, between the eyes. This feels like it is their central point and that everything else is peripheral to it. While our arms clearly feel that they are part of us, at the same time they feel as if they are external to that central point.

In developing the skills we need for meditation, it is very useful to become aware of this centre. It is then a good exercise to move your centre of attention around, and to experience how easy it is to do so.

The Awareness Exercise

And so to a simple exercise: Without moving, just close your eyes. Now imagine that you are in your kitchen. Imagine that you are really there and are looking at it through your own eyes. Look around at the kitchen and then walk over to the sink to get a glass of water. Take up the glass, fill it with water and then drink it. How does it feel?

Next, with your eyes still closed, imagine that you are in a busy city street. It is late on a Friday night. You have a dinner engagement that you must not be late for. There is a train to catch in a few minutes and there are people everywhere, jostling, bustling, hurrying. The noise, people bumping against you, the train to catch. How does it feel?

Next, take yourself in your mind to a favourite place in the countryside. A special place for you, a place of beauty and tranquility, a place that holds special memories, where you feel particularly close to nature. Walk slowly across the ground feeling the grass gentle underfoot. Look around at the trees and hear the wind gently blowing in the leaves. Look up at the blue sky and see an occasional white cloud drifting by. Feel the warm sun gently shining on your face. Allow the feeling of peace and tranquility to settle through. Again, how does it feel? Pause a moment and then open your eyes again.

This exercise has two advantages. It shows how, when you choose to think of busy things like the bustling city streets, you quickly feel bustled. You can feel the stress building up. As you dwell on tranquil things, that special place in nature, it has a gentle relaxing effect. You can feel relaxation taking place.

Moreover, the exercise shows how we can move our centre of awareness around. It takes little practice to really feel that we are in the kitchen, the city, or the countryside, rather than sitting here with our eyes closed.

B *Focussing on the body*

Now, instead of focussing on the city or the country, we will choose to concentrate on our body. We will move our centre of awareness into various muscle groups throughout the body, get to feel their level of relaxation, and then relax them more deeply, in fact completely.

To learn this level of control, we begin by focussing our attention on one group of muscles. The feet are a good place to begin. So take up your position for meditation, as described in the last chapter, and close your eyes.

Now move your centre of awareness, not to the city or the country, but down into your feet. You can begin to get the feel of this while you are reading. Imagine that you are 'in' your feet. What does it feel like? You may not feel much at first and this is where the technique will help you. For the first step is to contract all the muscles in the feet, really tense them up, make them stiff and tight. Now you can really appreciate the feeling of tension. Feels different to before, doesn't it? Tense the muscles for just a few seconds, long enough to really feel the tension. Then let them go. Let the muscles become soft and loose, like an old rag doll. Let go of all the tension, let the muscles relax completely.

Now you can feel what it is like to be relaxed. As the muscles relax, most people find that firstly they feel a warmth and a heaviness. Often they go on to feeling warm and light, a sign of deeper relaxation.

The technique, then, is to think in turn of each of the body's various muscle groups, to contract the muscles, and then to relax them. We start with the feet and move progressively on up through the calves, the thighs, and so on up to the head. Hence the name, Progressive Muscle Relaxation.

Now let's take the exercise a step further.

C   *Contracting and relaxing the muscles—a preparatory exercise*

The next skill we need to develop is the ability to contract and relax the muscle groups at will, to be able to think of the muscles in the feet, contract them and relax them, all the time holding our attention on the feeling this produces. First, have a practice session at contracting your muscles, the aim being simply to get used to contracting the muscles.

Now let's begin. This exercise is done best while seated in a chair but, if you prefer, it can also be done lying on your back on the floor.

Begin by taking up your symmetrical, slightly uncomfortable position and closing your eyes. You could sit next to a table so that you can open your eyes from time to time to check with the book's directions, you may prefer to memorise the instructions which are quite easy and straightforward, or have someone read them out for you.

Concentrate on your feet. Move your whole attention, your centre of awareness, down into them. Have all your concentration on your feet. Moving them a little may help you concentrate and feel in better touch with them. What do they feel like? Now contract the muscles of the feet. If it is difficult for you to do this, try curling your toes back towards your heels while at the same time stiffening them and resisting any movement. You are seeking to tense up all the muscles, making them tight and rigid. Now let the muscles relax — let them go. Imagine them now as being soft and loose like a rag doll.

You may need to be careful with your feet so that they do not develop a cramp. You only need to tighten them for a few seconds, long enough to appreciate the tension, then let them go.

Then on to the calves. Now we want to tighten the muscles in the calves, feel the tension, and let them go. If you have a bit of trouble getting these muscles to move, imagine you are at the beach and are trying to dig your toes into the sand. At the same time resist any movement. That will get the big muscles at the back of the calves working. You may find that there are muscles in other parts of the legs that want to get into the act and that you can feel them moving a bit too. That is all right, but just concentrate on the ones in the calves. As you practise, you probably will find that you can be more selective in your muscle control, but this is not particularly important. What is important is to be able to contract the muscles generally, feel the tension and release it, leaving the muscles feeling soft and loose.

Next we go up to the thighs which are the biggest muscle groups in the body. Just imagine lifting your feet up off the ground but at the same time holding them down with your hands; that really gets the big muscles in the top of the thighs contracting. You can really feel that tension. You can lift hard and feel the tension strongly. This will give you a good appreciation of what tension in these muscles is like. Then, when you relax them, you will find that they feel quite different. Soft and loose. Warm and heavy.

Now the buttocks: Imagine trying to lift yourself a bit higher in the seat. Contract the big muscles of the backside and lift yourself up a bit; then relax them. Remember, when you relax, to get that sense of relaxation right round the whole pelvic area — buttocks, hips, genital area, and the area inside the pelvis.

The tummy: Imagine that you are lying on your back and someone is about to drop a medicine ball on your tummy. This instinctively produces the right effect — you will contract the muscles at the front and the back at the same time. Now, as you relax, allow the feeling to be all through the tummy, the abdomen. No need to imagine a relaxed liver, intestine, etc., just that pervading feeling of deep relaxation — soft and loose, letting go.

The chest: This is a matter of bracing your chest like a barrel. Contract the chest muscles really tightly, like a drum — and let them go. Again, when you relax them, imagine that sense of relaxation right through the chest, the breasts as well. You will find it is easy to do once you practise a little.

The arms: Make them stiff like a board so that they resist movement in any direction. Make them really tight. And then relax them. Do them all in one go, from the shoulders right down to the ends of the fingers. You can leave the fingers out straight as they rest on your thighs, or you can gain extra emphasis by clenching the fingers into a fist. This really emphasises the feeling of tension. Also, in this preparatory exercise, you can gain a real appreciation of the relaxation by lifting your hands and shaking them a little — floppy, loose, like a rag doll. However, when it comes to doing the PMR exercise, it is probably better not to shake them physically.

The shoulders: Lift your shoulders up and pull your chin down. This not only contracts the big muscles at the top of the shoulders but also the muscles of the neck. When we say shoulders, it really means that whole shoulder-neck area.

The jaw: Grit your teeth. Clamping your jaw shut as tightly as you can is another good opportunity to get the feeling of what tension is really like. Remember to include the area around the front of the mouth as well. Crumple up your lips. As you relax, feel the tension releasing. Be aware of your tongue being relaxed also. Feel it becoming soft and loose. As it does so, it will probably feel a little larger.

The eyes: Close your eyes as firmly as you can. Then feel the sensation of relaxation across the bridge of the nose and around the eyes, as well as through the eyes themselves. Interestingly, we have had quite a few people in our groups who have found that their eyesight has improved so that they needed less prescription in their glasses. It seems for some, especially those with myopia, that as they relaxed more, their vision improved. Be aware of relaxing the whole area around the eyes, and have the feeling of relaxation through the eyes as well.

Finally, the forehead. Some people are better at frowning than others. Do the best you can. If you find it hard to frown you might like to lift your eyebrows up. Do which ever you feel comfortable with. Then let go. Have the sense of relaxation primarily in the forehead, but also across the top of the head.

Having now become used to the mechanics of contracting and relaxing the muscles in your body, we are ready for the next step — getting the attitude right.

Step 2—The Right State of Mind

As we have discussed before, no precise expectations are necessary. For many people, doing this exercise in a relaxed, easy manner does, in fact, lead them through physical relaxation into stillness of mind.

Know that at the very least the exercise is a pleasant one and it will help you to relax deeply. Just try it and see.

We are aiming in the long run to simply allow our mind to be still. That is a stated objective. But, to do that, we must aim not to try and make it happen! If we just go into it passively but purposefully, with a nice air of positive expectancy, then, in fact, things will start to happen. This is the essence of Integral Meditation.

As you are doing the PMR exercise, concentrate on how your body feels. As you feel more relaxed you will find that a feeling of warmth will come through it, and you will probably have a sensation of heaviness.

If, at any stage, you do find yourself thinking about something else, if you forget what you are doing or get distracted, just come back to the exercise and the words. Allow the words to direct your concentration again towards the feeling of the area that you are relaxing. Contract the muscles and let them go. Feel the relaxation, then move on to the next muscle group. Follow the directions of the words as they are spoken, or say them slowly to yourself, slowly, in an unemotional monotone. There should be a short quiet space between each group of words.

The aim is to just do it. Contract the muscles, relax them, and allow that feeling of relaxation and calm to be all through you. The words themselves are intended to be a bit vague. They are intended to accentuate feelings and the abstract, rather than to stimulate your intellect. Do not try to analyse them beyond the fact that they are designed to help move you away from active thinking into a more relaxed state of mind. The key words are 'letting go'. Letting go of physical tension, letting go of the emotions and of thought, letting go, just for a while. Just simply let go and allow yourself to be still.

When you get up to the forehead, take a few minutes to enjoy being still.

D *The Progressive Muscle Relaxation Exercise*

You can practise this basic and most useful technique in several ways:

1 Learn the steps by heart and lead yourself through them by repeating the words slowly and quietly to yourself.
2 Ask someone to read it to you – again slowly and softly in an unemotional monotone.

3 Use a tape recording. My cassettes are available (details at the end of this book), or you can record your own.

To repeat yet again, you need to practise until you can do it automatically, effortlessly, skilfully.

To begin with, allow yourself about fifteen to twenty minutes for this exercise.

Pause first, to remind yourself of the importance of your attitude. There should be no effort, no striving, no pushing in an effort to make something happen. Let's just do it, in an alert, passive manner and observe what happens.

In this exercise we will relax our muscles progressively, starting at the feet and working up to the forehead. We will do it by concentrating our attention on the muscles, contracting them, feeling the tension, then letting the tension go and feeling that relaxation, the letting go.

So, let's do it. Take up your position—symmetrical and slightly uncomfortable. Let your hands rest comfortably on your thighs.

Let your eyes close gently . . . Turn your thoughts inwards . . . And remember that this is a time for healing . . .

Now, really concentrate on your feet . . . Perhaps move them a little, really feel what they are like at the moment . . . Now, contract the muscles of the feet, feel the tension . . . And let them go . . . Feel the muscles relaxing . . . Feel the muscles becoming soft and loose . . . Feel it deeply . . . Completely . . . More and more . . . Letting go . . .

The calves . . . Contract the muscles, and let them go . . . Feel any tension relaxing . . . Soft and loose . . . Feel it deeply . . . It is a good feeling . . . A natural feeling . . . Feel the letting go . . .

The thighs . . . Contract the muscles, and let them go . . . Feel it all through . . . The legs feel warm and heavy . . . Soft and loose . . . More and more . . . Letting go . . .

The buttocks . . . Contract the muscles, and let them go . . . Deeply . . . Completely . . . More and more . . . Deeper and deeper . . . Letting go . . .

The tummy . . . Contract the muscles, and let them go . . . Feel it deeply . . . Calm and relaxed . . . Calm and relaxed . . .

Completely . . . More and more . . . All through . . . Letting go . . .

The chest . . . Contract the muscles, and let them go . . . Feel it all through . . . Relaxed . . . Relaxed . . . It is a good feeling . . . Feel the letting go . . .

The arms . . . Contract the muscles, and let them go . . . Feel it in the hands particularly . . . They feel warm and heavy . . . Soft and loose . . . More than relaxed . . . Letting go . . .

The shoulders . . . Contract the muscles, and let them go . . . Feel it deeply . . . Completely . . . Soft and loose . . . More and more . . . Deeper and deeper . . . Letting go . . .

The jaw . . . Contract the muscles, and let them go . . . Feel the jaw drop a little . . . Feel it deeply . . . Calm and relaxed . . . The tongue soft and loose . . . It is a good feeling . . . Feel the letting go . . .

The eyes . . . Contract the muscles, and let them go . . . Deeply . . . Completely . . . More and more . . . Letting go . . .

The forehead . . . Contract the muscles, and let them go . . . Feel the forehead smoothing out . . . Calm and relaxed . . . Feel it all through . . . More and more . . . Deeper and deeper . . . Letting go . . . Completely . . . Letting go . . . Completely calm and relaxed . . . Letting go . . . Deeply . . . Letting go . . . Letting go . . . Letting go . . .

If you are making your own tape, leave it silent here for as long as you like, and then finish with:

That's good . . . When you are ready, let your eyes gently open . . .

Many people find this exercise simple, direct and effective. Doing it leads to an immediate experience of feeling physically relaxed. This commonly leads on to a mental stillness that feels different to normal waking consciousness. This is the Relaxation Response, the first major step into the experience of Integral Meditation.

3 *Integral Meditation and the PMR Exercise*

When I began teaching meditation, all I used was this technique based on the PMR Exercise. Most people in a group setting found on their first attempt that it led them directly into feeling deeply physically relaxed, they experienced the Relaxation Response.

For about one in ten of participants, the sense of physical relaxation was followed within a few days by experiencing a stillness of mind. A few even found it on the first day. These people felt that they were more than just relaxed, they were meditating. Meditation began for them where the Relaxation Response left off. From feeling physically relaxed they moved into an experience of profound inner stillness. This is Integral Meditation.

After a few weeks, most people in the groups were reporting positive changes in their lives which they attributed to the exercise. Usually about one in ten did not follow through, but dropped out. It was usual for a large percentage of the group to have problems with stilling their thoughts and some became quite frustrated.

In those early years of teaching, everyone who persevered eventually felt satisfied with their experience of meditation. For some, 'eventually' meant several months, or more. Remember, for me it had taken two and a half years – although, in the meantime, the practice had been instrumental in helping me to overcome cancer! Something practical was happening along the way.

Over the years it has been possible to recognise the common problems and obstacles and to introduce new strategies to overcome them more easily and quickly.

Also, in the groups, the gradient of experience and benefit soon became apparent. As soon as people learned to relax physically and were able to remain physically still, benefits from the Relaxation Response began to flow.

I still see this regularly when new people in a group express their concerns about being completely unable to still their minds.

One such person was Andrew W. who had recently been diagnosed with cancer. Dragged somewhat unwillingly to the groups by his wife, he became enthusiastic about meditation. Being a businessman with an active brain, he found he could practise the physical relaxation and remain physically still for long periods, but then he seemed to be beset by a constant stream of irrelevant thoughts. After six weeks he decried himself as a hopeless case, saying he doubted if he could ever get anywhere with meditation. I asked him if he had noticed any changes over those six weeks. He thought for a moment.

'Well, now you mention it', were his words, 'I have been sleeping a whole lot better'. His wife quickly added that several months ago he had been so distressed that he was sleeping only one or two hours a night and was so restless that she had moved to a separate bed. 'Last night', she said, 'he slept for seven hours, the longest continuous sleep he has had for months and I have been noticing he has stopped thrashing about all night'.

'Yes', Andrew continued, 'and now that you mention it, I was at the radiotherapist's a few days ago and he asked me what I was doing, because apparently I am responding to treatment much better than he expected. And, oh' he added, almost as an afterthought, 'I am feeling a whole lot better'.

The rest of the group laughed heartily at our self-confessed 'hopeless' meditator who was experiencing so many positive 'coincidences'. On further questioning, Andrew felt sure that these changes were directly related to his practice. He was experiencing the immediate benefits of the Relaxation Response. He felt a renewed enthusiasm to continue with it and we discussed other techniques he could practise to enable him to move on into meditation.

So, for some, the learning process is easy; for others it takes perseverance, practice, and possibly the learning of some extra techniques.

We will discuss these techniques further in the next chapter but first let us consider what to do next if the initial PMR Exercise is working well for you.

4 Simplifying the PMR Exercise: a quick path to the Relaxation Response and Integral Meditation

Many beginners find the PMR Exercise a satisfying basis for further meditation. They are keen to keep practising, using this basic form of Integral Meditation as their pathway into deeper meditation. Many need nothing more.

I certainly recommend this exercise as an ideal place to start. If you practise it and are content to keep going with it, you can develop it a little more by learning some more skills.

If at any stage you become deeply frustrated with the PMR Exercise, read the next chapter again and reconsider your options. Usually such frustrations spring from inner chatter, the restless, thinking mind, and there are many ways of dealing with this if it gets out of control.

But, to repeat, if you are content with your progress with Integral

Meditation, be patient, keep it simple, keep practising, and push on.

You can simplify the PMR Exercise, put less emphasis on the technique and so come closer to being able to meditate using the Direct Approach. You can simplify the technique, wean yourself off the technique, and gently drop it.

5   *The PMR Exercise without contracting the muscles*

As the next step in Integral Meditation, try repeating the basic PMR Exercise, only this time do not contract the muscles first. Just think of each muscle group and consciously relax each area.

Having a good experience of deep physical relaxation via the PMR Exercise before moving on to this step is a great advantage. You will have experienced what it feels like to be deeply relaxed, will be able to recall the feeling, let go again, and recapture that feeling.

For most people this feeling is one of the muscles releasing tension, letting go. As they do so, they feel they are slowly expanding, like a compressed spring being gently released. Often this is accompanied by a sensation of warmth. Sometimes there is a transitory tingling, often a sense of heaviness. As the relaxation goes deeper, there is a feeling of lightness.

Commonly, as this feeling of lightness settles over the body, if the mind does not attempt to evaluate or question the feeling but flows along with it, just letting it happen, letting it flow and spread, then the mind will, in fact, become still.

Using the PMR Exercise without contracting the muscles first makes it easier for the exercise to flow. There is less to think about, such as which muscles to contract next. You can just let it progress more automatically, more skilfully, more simply.

In practising this exercise, you may find it works some days but not on others. Sometimes you may need to return to the contracting of the muscles, to focus your attention, to lead you away from your everyday thoughts.

It is always important to take the feeling of physical relaxation to a deep level. You can relax physically without meditating, but it is virtually impossible to meditate well without physically relaxing. (You can move physically in meditation, but still you must be relaxed to do it.) With any method, you need to be able to relax physically.

As you practise Integral Meditation using the PMR Exercise without muscle contraction, you should find you can get that same degree of physical relaxation and that the technique also leads you into a mental stillness.

6 *The PMR Wave*

Having practised the PMR Exercise without contracting the muscles, and finding that effective, you can take it another step further.

Now, instead of thinking of the feet relaxing, then the calves, then the thighs, consider the legs as a whole unit. You may like to begin with one leg at a time although often they can be done together.

Just feel the legs relaxing, letting go, soft and loose, all through, deeply relaxed and calm, letting go.

Then do the same with the body parts — buttocks, tummy, chest, arms and shoulders. All as one unit, letting go.

Then the head, again one unit, relaxing deeply, completely, letting go.

For this exercise, some people find it easier to reverse the order. They start with relaxing the head muscles, letting them go, and then feel a wave of relaxation move downwards through their body.

7 *Back to the Direct Method*

For some, with practice, this allows them to sit down, close their eyes and feel a wave of relaxation and calm moving right through their body. With this sensation, their mind turns inwards, away from the mundane things of life, and they enter rapidly into the stillness of meditation. At this point they are virtually using no technique, although they are using a lot of skill.

This is the Direct Method, a method worth working towards — not striving for, but working consciously and purposefully towards. We know what we want to have happen, and we know that if it is to happen we need to not try to make it happen.

A reminder

Remember that as soon as you can relax physically and sit still formally for even ten to twenty minutes, you will start to gain benefit. It is a great help to be assured that when you are in this physically relaxed state, even if your mind is active, as long as you are content for it to be active and do not get frustrated or worried by it, you will be releasing tension and allowing your body chemistry to balance itself. As you practise you will find that, in fact, you are experiencing the Relaxation Response. That experience will lead to the many health related benefits we have discussed.

If you are seeking relief from stress, or to manage an illness, that may be all you need to do.

If you persevere with Integral Meditation, you can be virtually assured that sooner or later you will experience the state that often seems so elusive — the mental stillness that carries extra benefits with it.

If personal development and spiritual reality is what you seek, you may well find that the simple but profound stillness provides you with all the answers.

However, if at any stage you feel frustrated, unsatisfied or blocked in your progress, and this feeling persists unduly, then Chapter Six is for you.

Before going on to explore these other options, let us investigate how we can bring the experience of formal Integral Meditation, and its benefits, into our daily life.

Chapter Five

MEDITATION IN ACTION

Having now established a basic Health Meditation technique, Integral Meditation, how can we gain the best from the technique? How can we take its benefits into our daily life experience?

Happily, many people find that the initial PMR technique does lead them into a good experience of the Relaxation Response and on deeper into the stillness of Integral Meditation. Once this occurs, many of the benefits of meditation begin to flow spontaneously without any extra effort.

Speeding up the technique

For greatest efficiency and so we can derive full benefit from the technique, there are some extra practices recommended.

Already, we have discussed the advantages of speeding up the actual technique. Beginning with the formal process of contracting muscles and relaxing them, and moving progressively up through the muscle groups of the body, is an ideal starting point. Just let me reinforce the fact that the simpler and less complicated the technique the better. So in time, progressing at a comfortable pace, it is well worthwhile dropping off the muscle contraction and working towards that Direct Method.

Also, you can increase the depth and efficacy of your meditation using the techniques that follow.

Practice in more challenging situations

(i) *More uncomfortable positions*

When you are beginning to learn, being in an ideal environment, tranquil, calm and surrounded by a supportive group, makes initial progress far easier. As you establish your practice you will begin to develop some skill at it; it will start to flow for you.

Now if you take up a more uncomfortable position or sit in a more distracting environment, you will test your skills and develop them.

In fact many of the traditional meditation techniques use painful positions as a calculated way to do this. For our needs, however, particularly for Health Meditation, it is important not to exceed what is a reasonable degree of pain for you. Unless you can transcend the discomfort fairly quickly, it is only going to stress you and defeat the purpose.

At the same time, the judicious use of discomfort remains a valuable tool. When you begin, if you are aware of a degree of discomfort, then to relax enough to overcome it and to enter into the Relaxation Response and Integral Meditation, you will need to sharpen your concentration and your ability to be the impartial observer. We will come to specific techniques to develop these two qualities shortly.

It makes good sense, therefore, to begin your meditation using a relatively easy, just slightly uncomfortable position. Then, as time goes on and your skills improve, move into the more advanced, more uncomfortable positions.

Now, I know that if I lie down it is a great way to relax and revive a tired body, but the quality of actual meditation is much better when I sit on the floor. It has, however, taken many years of practice for me to be able to sit still for an hour, cross-legged on the floor. During the early years, using a sitting or lying position was effective in meeting my needs. There just has been a natural progression and development.

(ii)   *More distracting locations*

Of more immediate value, is the move to practise in noisier, more distracting situations. This really does develop your concentration, your 'observer' qualities. This teaches selective concentration and the ability to remain calm in potentially disturbing, stressful situations. It will help you to take the benefits of the formal meditation practice into your daily life experience.

So be prepared to meditate where there is traffic noise, at least on some occasions. Be prepared to let the noise come and go. At first you may be very aware of it, you may say to yourself, 'There goes a truck, there goes a noisy car', etc. When such noises come into your awareness, just let them come and let them go. Choose not to react. Do not fight them, do not try to block them out. Resist the temptation to indulge in becoming angry. Just let them be there. Similarly in your home environment. Once you have reached a degree of proficiency it is actually helpful to have some intermittent noise.

Curiously, this 'letting go' is an extremely effective way to become unaware of distractions, both internal and external! If you give them no attention, if you do not react to them, they simply become unimportant, they simply fade away. You will find that they cease to come into your awareness and you will settle into stillness.

The fact is, this stillness is always there, it is always inside us. Everything else, every noise or thought, is added to it. If we just let the distractions go, we will return to an experience of the common, underlying factor, that simple yet profound stillness within.

This may take a little practice and willpower at first, but once you have experienced it, you will be more confident of its effectiveness.

Having developed your skills in these formal practice sessions, it is then time to take them into your daily experience. Again, when your practice is regular and effective, a lot of this will occur spontaneously without the need for conscious effort. But here, too, we can identify what works and use our conscious mind to direct the development of further skills.

Using the Relaxation Response in daily life

To maintain our equilibrium, our balance, our health, we should aim to maintain as relaxed a state as possible. Remember the stress cycle, the negative effects of the prolonged stimulation of the Fight-or-Flight Response and the balancing effect of the Relaxation Response.

We can regain our balance using the formal practice of the Relaxation Response and Integral Meditation. To maintain this sense of balance, this poise, we can become aware of developing and maintaining a relaxed state all through the day.

Again, to be relaxed is not to be slack. To be relaxed is to be free to respond to the needs of the moment, to be able to use just the right amount of energy required for the task in hand.

To redevelop this skill, begin by practising the Relaxation Response regularly through the day. Here red traffic lights are a real gift!

Program yourself so that every time you stop at a red traffic light you will feel the Relaxation Response, that wave of relaxation, flow right through your body. Having practised the physical relaxation exercise during your formal meditation periods, you will be skilled at it and it will flow easily. Initially, you may need to close your eyes momentarily to focus your attention on your body. As you practise more, you will be able to turn your thoughts inwards and do what is like an internal, physical inventory.

Move your awareness, your attention through your body, relaxing and releasing any tension. Feel the muscles becoming soft and loose while maintaining that alert attitude that leaves you knowing that you will not be slack or sleepy but, in fact, more efficient, free of stress and tension, more able to respond appropriately.

You might like to repeat this process at other times when you have a few moments to spare. Before appointments is a good opportunity and before meals is highly recommended. Take time to regain that feeling of being relaxed, let the calm be with you. Not only will you feel better, but your digestion will appreciate it, too.

Trigger areas

As you practise this, you may find that one or two of your particular muscle groups are more likely to record tension when you are under stress. Frequently this will be the shoulders, the forehead, the jaw or the hands. People vary. If you have one area that accentuates your stress, call it your trigger area. Its value is that usually, if you can relax that area, it will trigger relaxation throughout your body. The trigger area is like a key to your relaxation.

If you do have a trigger area, concentrate on relaxing it regularly through the day. Say your trigger area is in your shoulder region. Before you get up is a good time to check through your body and make sure you are starting the day physically relaxed. Chances are, that when you first begin all this, by the time you are up out of bed you will notice your shoulders are tight. You relax them, but then by the time you have gone to the toilet, there they are tight again. Relax them. Probably after the shower, tight again. Relax again. And so it goes on. You need to practise. To recondition your body, to recondition your self into being relaxed. You will need to avoid the temptation to become frustrated with this. Be prepared to work at it, to be patient.

When many people begin relaxation and meditation they discover just how tense their body has been in the past, how they had become accustomed to it and taken it to be their normal state. The experience of deep relaxation is therefore often followed by comments about how good my body feels, how pleasant it is to actually feel relaxed.

I say that this is the joy of feeling normal!

Tension in the body generally, or in the trigger areas specifically, sometimes can be deeply entrenched and hard to get free of. Here massage, and possibly manipulation, can be a great aid. Massage is a natural complement to good relaxation and meditation. It is a pleasure to give and to receive. Happily, there are many good masseurs around now, as the value of massage is being well recognised. So if you do have trouble relaxing, massage can be a natural ally.

Relaxed activity

The next step is to maintain the sense of calm and relaxation felt in meditation and hold on to it while doing your daily tasks.

This is the ideal. To let the effect of the meditation flow into your daily life. Again, if your practice is regular, deep and effective, this will happen spontaneously. But here, too, you can choose to work at it.

Firstly, practise this extra skill in a formal way. When you are sitting in meditation, begin by gently opening your eyes, maintaining the feeling of calm and relaxation. If you lose it, close your eyes again, let yourself settle back into that still state, then open your eyes again.

If you are deeply relaxed, you may well find that what you see is rather curious! In a deep meditative state, your sight will (temporarily while you do this exercise) regress to a simpler function. You will see in black and white! This is actually a good way of getting feedback.

I particularly enjoy doing this outside, lying under a tree on a sunny day. When you meditate and then open your eyes, you will see the leaves, swaying gently in the breeze, in black and white. In fact, if you are deeply into it, you will see the white more as silver, shining and sparkling, and the black more like holes, a real absence of colour. The effect is quite magical and just very pleasant to behold.

Naturally you would not look directly into the sun during this exercise.

Of course, if you try and 'look at' this effect too hard, it goes instantly. Here again, good feedback. It will help you to develop the skill of selective concentration and to be aware of what works for you.

In a more practical sense, you can then practise getting up from your meditation, taking the feeling with you. This is an important step as your practice progresses. Do not feel that the formal periods are the only times to be relaxed and when you may experience that calm. Take the feeling with you and allow it to be with you all day.

So be conscious of the calm attitude when firstly you are doing simple mundane things like washing the dishes. Concentrate your attention on what you are doing, let go of other thoughts, be there with the dishes, doing them in a relaxed, calm manner. Then try it when preparing a meal or driving the car. Alert but relaxed, really doing it and with that sense of calm poise.

Be gentle with yourself

Now again, this may take some practice. Allow it to develop, be patient. Resist that temptation to get frustrated or angry with yourself. It does take time to change ingrained habits and if you have a history of being tense or overly emotional it will take some commitment and perseverance to change it. It can be done. Work at it at a comfortable pace for you. Take delight when you see the changes coming. They may be small at first, they may be dramatic. Be assured that they will come, you can do it!

Perhaps the most wonderful thing in all this is just how often it does work and how dramatic the benefits have been for so many people. Herein lies another potential trap for young players! (Old ones, too, I imagine.)

Ups and downs

Learning to meditate can often be like a traditional honeymoon. First, there is the excitement of doing something new, there is an element of adventure, you just do it and enjoy it. It all happens easily, smoothly, joyously. There is an air of magic and euphoria.

Often, however, it seems this wonderful high precedes a let-down.

Back from the honeymoon, you start to analyse. It was so good, how did it happen? Will it be that good again? How will this new part of my life fit in with the old? What can I do to improve it?

You start thinking about it. The spontaneity is gone. Soon, too, the magic. Now the hard work begins. Now the need to nurture and develop this precious part of life.

Often the first experience of Integral Meditation leads to a wonderful experience. Regularly, in the first week or two, beginners tell me of the joy and delight they are gaining from their meditation and how much benefit they are feeling from it. These people have usually practised the Progressive Muscle Relaxation, adopted a passive approach, just done it, and felt something happen. Not only the Relaxation Response, but a hint of stillness. Perhaps just a glimpse, a flicker. Perhaps something more. But, in that glimpse, there is a flash of awareness, an inkling that in that stillness lie profound and satisfying answers, that there is something far more on offer here than just physical relaxation and health. There is the hint of a higher state of consciousness, a feeling like coming home, home to the real centre where direct knowing will lead to an appreciation of what, in fact, is real.

This inkling of the value of entering that stillness often leads to a great desire, an urgent passion to experience it more deeply. Frequently this sense of urgency is compounded by a patient whose understanding of meditation has been that the healing only flows from this self-same stillness — 'I must get it right!', they say. The quest for the still mind is on, with great fervour!

Then, not uncommonly, there rapidly follows a slump, a descent from the high into what seems like an unsatisfactory experience falling far short of what might be possible.

Of course, if all you are seeking is stress relief or health management, this quest for higher states of consciousness may be irrelevant. You may be quite content to relax physically and let the mind be calm. This being so, you make no extra effort, and you may experience these other states quite effortlessly, as a by-product of your practice!

In general, it is noticeable that people who just have a casual interest in meditation or who are interested in using it for personal development, report more rapid progress. An understanding of why this is so helps the others to avoid the obstacles.

Many beginners have found that the sense of striving created a barrier to what they were seeking. The striving, the lure of this special something, led to effort, tension, frustration. At the same time as they were striving, the desire to assess progress has helped build obstacles across the path leading into the stillness.

It is not uncommon, therefore, for beginners to have a good initial experience. Like the honeymoon, it all seems natural, simple and easy. They just do it and it flows. Then come the thoughts — Wow! What's happening? How can I do it again? How can I do it better? Oh no, it doesn't seem the same this time — it's different now. Is something wrong? What did I do?

Frequently these attempts to 'make it happen' and to assess progress are at the core of the slump that is commonly seen a few weeks or months after a beginner takes up meditation.

Often, for unaided meditators, getting back to that same sense of magic, that feeling of 'doing it right' that was there in the early days, has taken many months or even years. Do not forget that in Zen tradition, twenty years, even in that highly dedicated and experienced meditation school, is considered a reasonable time to take to reach these higher states. If we can presume to do it in a year or two, let alone months or even weeks — !! Perhaps the most amazing thing I have observed in all my work is the large number of people who actually do meditate well and quickly. For many, however, there is a need for understanding and patience.

When all else fails, read the instructions!

The value of our intellect is that we can use it to gain an understanding of the process. Once we know what is desired and what happens, we can work our way through it. The intellect has to be transcended in meditation, but, used wisely, it can help us to save a lot of time and smooth out the whole process. It makes a good stepping-stone.

So, let us pause to consider a little more theory and to examine the principles behind traditional meditation techniques. This will add to our understanding of why Integral Meditation is so effective and explain what to do if it happens that this exercise is not completely effective for you.

To reiterate, traditionally, meditation was seen as a means of seeking a direct experience of a higher state of consciousness.

Remember that this state is characterised by physical relaxation combined with an alert, still mind.

We have already identified the four elements required to enter this state. Again, they are:

1 A symmetrical, slightly uncomfortable position
2 A means of physical relaxation
3 The quality of passive observation
4 A shift in conscious awareness

Also we have discussed the ways of translating these steps into practice, into a pathway to meditation we have called Integral Meditation.

How to Meditate

(a) *Use no method*

The desired state being one of stillness, really there is nothing to do! We just need to be still. In practice this is not so easy, so many people need a method that allows them to learn to practise and develop the skill of simply being still.

(b) *Using a method*

Again our aim is to be still, so the simplest effective technique is the one for us to seek out and to use. We may have to experiment a little to find the best approach for us. An experienced teacher may well save a lot of time.

Once we know what is required, however, we can at least start at the simplest point and move on to other approaches if and when they are needed.

Again, if we need to use a method, we will always firstly require a means of relaxing physically. We then need a means of stilling the mind. If we do this with the alert, passive observing quality we have discussed, we should rapidly enter meditation.

So, to summarise:

The principles of meditation methods:

1 Relaxing Physically

The PMR exercise is excellent for this.

2   Stilling the Mind

Most approaches utilise two elements:

(a)   *Some method of concentration*

This is the *activity* that is used. Focussing the attention facilitates the transition from random thoughts into the entering of stillness.

(b)   *Develop an attitude like an impartial observer*

This is the *attitude* that is adopted.

You can see from this that Integral Meditation combines all these requisites in a simple, easily learned process. Beginning with the PMR exercise, you contract and relax the muscles, you concentrate on the feeling of relaxation. As your body relaxes, there is a reflex relaxation in the mind. At the same time you allow yourself to observe outside sounds or inner thoughts. Like watching the white clouds pass by on a blue sky, they come when they want to, and they go when they want to. You are the impartial observer. Soon they cease to come. There is a whole lot more blue sky! You enter the stillness.

For many this is enough. Learning Integral Meditation and refining it, simplifying it as time goes on, is fully satisfying.

For those needing more help, the next chapter will elaborate on these principles some more, and investigate what can be done if so far the techniques are not working for you.

Chapter Six

STILLING THE RESTLESS MIND

What we have discussed so far works for many people, but not for all. No problem!

Obviously Integral Meditation is not the only way to enter meditation. While it is a very simple and effective approach, it does not suit everyone.

Most people do find it a reliable way to learn how to relax physically. If you experience that relaxation and are then prepared to practise, to let your thoughts come and go and to patiently await stiller states, then please do just that.

If, however, you reach the point of frustration, if thoughts seem endless and your practice unsatisfactory, do not despair. There are other options available.

To make sense of these options, let us go back to the Principles of Meditation Methods. The need for relaxing physically is always there. Now by expanding our understanding of how to still the mind we will be able to understand the role of the great variety of other techniques.

The principles of techniques for stilling the mind

The basic tools are concentration and observation.

1 Concentration

If you need to do something to be still, then this is the activity to engage in! The type of concentration you use should be chosen to meet your needs. Some people find that their mind can be stilled by focussing on one simple thing; others find that they need quite an elaborate structure to work with.

Simple concentration techniques focus on simple subjects which are usually rhythmical in nature. Examples would be to concentrate on the natural rhythm of breathing, or on the repetition of one word, over and over as in the use of a mantra. Alternatively, you could concentrate on one simple subject like a candle.

Complex concentration techniques obviously are more involved. Examples would be concentrating on the PMR exercise, or concentrating on a detailed imagery exercise such as fantasising walking through an imagined country scene.

Another option is to simply concentrate on being aware of whatever happens. The idea is to simply concentrate upon observing, without assessment or reaction. The aim is to simply be aware of just whatever is presenting for you at the moment. This is really concentrating on being an impartial observer, as we have already discussed.

Now to elaborate further.

2   Observation

This is the attitude to be developed in meditation. It is really a state of discriminating alertness, being aware of what is happening in a focussed, selective manner. In other words, not lapsing into a mindless reverie but adopting a mindful attitude, a keen alert awareness of what is happening. Still but alert. Mindful, not mindless. An attitude that is free from assessment or reaction.

The Mindful Impartial Observer.

Even here there are options. There are two basic ways in which to approach this attitude:

(a)   *The Passive Approach*

This requires no intention other than to see what happens. It is the attitude we discussed for commencing Health Meditation and is quite unstructured. External sounds or feelings are recorded, observed, not reacted to or assessed, just observed — allowed to come and go as they occur. Internal thoughts likewise are free to come and go as they arise. Again, they are observed and let go, just like watching the white clouds pass by on a blue sky.

(b) *The Analytical Approach*

Here the intention is to find out more about your thoughts, where they come from, what their nature is and what they lead to. This is the essence of Insight Meditation, the process of getting to know yourself better. What am I? What could I be? What is the nature of reality? Techniques based on this approach are all highly structured.

Putting it together

All meditation techniques are based upon a combination of the activity of concentration, overlaid with the attitude of being an observer.

Again, Health Meditation relies for its effects on being kept simple. The form of Health Meditation we have concentrated upon, Integral Meditation, is in principle very easy. Especially its early stages, characterised by the Relaxation Response, are very easy to learn and to practise effectively. This type of meditation reliably discharges inner tension and removes the effects of chronic stress. With time, it spontaneously leads to many positive life changes occurring. Old negative patterns fall away, a positive life pattern emerges. The inner healer is liberated.

More advanced meditation techniques like Insight meditation take more practice and can be quite hard work, requiring perseverance and a good sense of humour! This type of meditation aims to utilise a subtle level of consciousness to provide an insight into the nature of reality — directly and intuitively. This type of meditation does not lead to such immediate and impressive physical health benefits but does do wonders for your state of mind.

Being aware of all this, let us now get practical again. How do we utilise this knowledge to establish effective meditation? What should we do?

I am using repetition to reinforce these basic principles, to clarify them and extend our understanding. This will enable us to apply the principles practically and to use them with skill.

How to meditate—a practical overview of the choices

1 *The direct approach—use no method : just simply be still*

A good ideal but may be too simple to begin with!

2   *Use a method*

(a)   *Relax physically : using the PMR exercise (see Chapter Four)*

(b)   *Still the mind*

    (i)   Use the PMR exercise as an aid

        a)   Concentrate on the PMR exercise and the feeling of relaxation

        b)   Adopt the attitude of an impartial observer allowing any distracting sounds or thoughts to come and go

        c)   If disturbed, concentrate again on relaxing the body

        d)   Allow yourself to move on into stillness, there is nothing more that needs to be done, just go with it, let it happen

        e)   Persevere while you feel like progress is being made

        f)   If you get frustrated, or feel like you are at a dead end, particularly with persistent unwanted thoughts, then -

    (ii)   Utilise a secondary focus to concentrate upon

        a)   Choose another focus for your attention

        b)   This will lead you away from random, distracting thoughts and focus your attention on one thing

        c)   Maintain the stance of a Passive Observer

        d)   As you maintain your concentration, you will move beyond it, into stillness

        e)   The secondary focus gradually becomes unnecessary.

3   *You simplify the method and work back to the direct approach*

Integral Meditation and beyond

So again, the **direct approach** is the simplest and best if you can do it that simply. If you need a method, the process incorporating 2 a) and b) (i) – a) to e), is what we described as Integral Meditation and this is recommended as an ideal starting point.

If that method does not seem satisfactory for you, there are two skills to work on – being a better Observer and applying better Concentration. Practising these skills will help establish more satisfying and effective meditation.

1 Becoming the impartial observer

A common experience for people who sit to relax or meditate is that they become aware that they are thinking. This is not as foolish a statement as it may at first sound.

Normally we are so busy thinking and are so caught up with our thoughts that we are just doing it, it is just happening. This is like our analogy of watching a movie that has our full attention. We can become so caught up by the action that we lose any awareness of being in a picture theatre watching a screen. For a time we live in the fantasy of actually being in that movie. It is as though we are a part of it.

Contrast with this the experience of watching a boring movie. It is easy to sit back and be very aware that you are in a theatre, that you are watching a movie, seeing the pictures go around, hearing the sound and being quite consciously the impartial observer merely recording what is happening.

This latter approach, being the impartial observer, is an excellent way to deal with the thoughts that pass by in meditation.

The analogy of observing traffic passing by is a very useful one to return to. If you are looking through a window on to a busy highway, it is relatively easy to be an impartial observer and to merely record what is happening. There goes a green Holden, a blue Ford, a motor bike, a truck, and so on. No comment, no judgment. Pure observation. Being mindful of what is happening.

Of course, what can happen is that you see that red Ferrari go by and start to fantasise! 'Gee, I like that one. I could see myself . . .'. Or a motor bike goes by: 'No, I can't see myself on that ...'. As soon as judgment or fantasy comes into it, the exercise is lost.

In meditation, allowing your thoughts to come and go, merely observing them pass by, has a remarkable effect. Firstly, you find that the traffic begins to slow down. Instead of a constant, steady stream of thoughts, you will find you become more aware of each thought, that they seem to be passing more slowly and that there are small gaps of stillness between the individual thoughts. It is like the difference between peak hour traffic and a quiet afternoon.

Developing this quality of being the observer will allow you to move on to being quite unaffected by thoughts, to being able to retain that basic calm even if thoughts are passing by.

At a Zen retreat, the master of some thirty years standing was asked if he ever had thoughts enter his head while he was meditating. He laughed heartily and replied, 'Doesn't everyone? For me', he said, 'the thoughts come when they are ready, and they go when they are ready. They do not affect me. They pass by like white clouds drifting across a blue sky. Thoughts are not a problem'. 'Then, did he experience moments of real stillness?' he was asked. 'Yes, but they retained the air of special moments, like a precious gift.' Surprisingly to some, he added that they carried no extra emphasis. The important thing was to practise and to experience, to observe what happened. For him, out of this practice came all that was necessary.

Exercises in observing

One can practise this quality of being the impartial observer using the following exercises. Please note that these techniques can also be used as a basis for Insight Meditation, the practice of which we will be examining in the next chapter.

(i)   The watch exercise

This is something of a play on words. It involves watching the sweep second hand of a watch as it moves around a clock face. The aim is to remain focussed on observing the sweep hand moving around, all the while being aware that you are watching it and not thinking of anything else. It is a challenging exercise and, if you have not done it before, two minutes is usually plenty to begin with. Try it, and see how you go. Be prepared to be gentle with yourself. When you realise you are thinking of something else, return to the 'watching' exercise.

It is useful to retain your sense of humour and laugh at the difficult nature of the exercise. Think of your mind as being like a wayward, mischievous child which needs some gentle discipline and direction. However, the exercise is a powerful tool to help develop the 'observer' quality, and your ability to concentrate.

(ii)   Sit and observe traffic

As already discussed, watching a busy road and just observing the cars go by is a useful exercise. The task is to observe and record — not to assess or judge or think of other things. Of course, you can take up this attitude with any part of your day and practise observing—not assessing or judging, just aiming to observe what is really happening.

(iii) Fantasise

Another technique to develop the observer quality begins with sitting and relaxing physically. The PMR Exercise is ideal for this. Then imagine your thoughts as being like white clouds drifting across a blue sky. If your imagination is good, you may see your thoughts written on the clouds, drifting by as if a signwriter has been. Another possibility is to imagine that you are sitting on the bank of a river observing the thoughts being like logs or pieces of stick drifting past. Again you may 'see' your thoughts written on or contained within the logs.

Still another version of this exercise is to imagine that you are comfortably settled in the stillness at the bottom of the ocean. As you sit there, thoughts arise like bubbles. You 'see' the thoughts contained within the bubbles and watch them gently rising and gradually drifting to the surface to disperse into the air.

(iv) Observe your natural thoughts

I recommend that everyone should at least try this. We have discussed it a good deal already. It is what I find the best and easiest approach for me and, being the simplest, it is very effective. After the PMR Exercise, aim to be content to let your thoughts come and go. It's okay to be thinking. Just let the thoughts come and go. Watch them. Watch them like an impartial observer. Observe them like the cars passing in the street or the white clouds drifting by on the blue sky. Let them come when they want, be aware of them and let them go when they want. No need to resist them, react to them, just let them come and go. The benefit is that they get bored and give up! Thoughts love an audience and if no one takes any interest, they just stop coming. The flow slows down, the moments of stillness between them get longer, and soon you will find yourself free of them—for a while, at least.

Adding the attitude of the Impartial Observer to the technique of the PMR exercise makes an ideal combination. Again, this is what I call Integral Meditation. It acts as a reliable stepping stone into the deep stillness of meditation. Also, this approach can readily be simplified to become the Direct Method.

Identifying the simplicity and effectiveness of this method for Health Meditation stands to the credit and memory of Dr Ainslie Meares. This approach continues to be the one I recommend as the starting point and it is ideal for ongoing practice.

2   Concentration

For some — quite a few, in fact — the thoughts keep rolling on, and on, and on! They seem unceasing, and not infrequently they produce frustration and worry. These judgments in response to the thoughts, the reactions to the frustration and worry, are the problem. The thoughts would be okay, they would not be significant, if you did not react to them. The reaction of frustration or concern is the problem.

In practical terms, if you are reacting, if you are feeling frustrated or worried by the apparent lack of success, a more structured form of concentration is probably what you need to adopt. You can use a concentration technique like a stepping stone, a useful means of learning. Once you have mastered it, again, the idea will be to simplify it and work back to that basic Direct Method.

Interestingly, structured concentration techniques have been the starting point for most of the world's traditional meditation

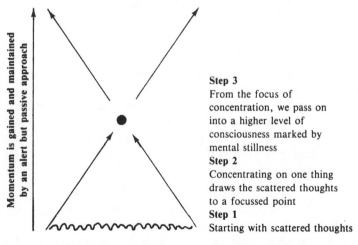

Step 3
From the focus of concentration, we pass on into a higher level of consciousness marked by mental stillness
Step 2
Concentrating on one thing draws the scattered thoughts to a focussed point
Step 1
Starting with scattered thoughts

Momentum is gained and maintained by an alert but passive approach

Focussing Scattered Thoughts—using Concentration

techniques. Instead of allowing the thoughts to come and go as they please and to observe them doing so, they chose one particular focus for concentration. The aim was to think of that one thing and nothing else.

It is a little like holding a lens out in the rays of the sun and, in doing so, concentrating their energy on one point. By concentrating on one thing, scattered thoughts are focussed and from this point of focussed concentration, the mind opens out into the experience of stillness. This can be represented diagrammatically:

Stilling the mind via Concentration

Not surprisingly, stages can be identified in this process of moving from normal, waking conscious awareness, through concentration, into stillness. In fact, there is a clearly defined five-step process involved. Virtually all the communities and religions of the world have used this process at some time. The whole process, and its various parts, have been referred to as 'meditation' by different commentators and this is why there has been confusion over the definition of meditation as it is used in our present-day language. In this traditional sense, meditation was described as being only one of the five steps in the process while today, popular usage of that term is generally somewhat different.

The traditional five steps, however, were Concentration, Meditation, Contemplation, Unification, Illumination. Being aware of these steps is another real aid in developing our practice. We will look at the principles first, then explore techniques that utilise them.

The five step process

Relaxation (Can be incorporated into Concentration)

Frequently, though not always, there was a distinct relaxation phase. The PMR Exercise, for example, is a classic yoga technique. Other exercises, especially those based upon breathing, were commonly used.

Frequently then, physical relaxation was incorporated into the first part of the exercise and used to help focus the concentration. Often, in fact, relaxation was used as the focus for the concentration.

1   Concentration

Just about anything and everything has been used in attempts to focus and hold the thoughts on one thing and one thing only. The fact is that concentration is hard work and takes plenty of practice. Most people find that at first a few minutes of undivided concentration is all they can manage before their attention begins to wander. It can take quite a while to tame the mind which is like a playful wild horse, keen to keep its freedom and often bucking at discipline.

Looking at the general themes used for concentration, we can identify four major groups — sounds, thoughts, actions, and objects.

Whatever the nature of the focus for concentration, the aim was to think of that focus and nothing else. Once this was achieved, meditation was under way.

2   Meditation

Meditation traditionally was the ability to concentrate on one thing to the exclusion of all other thoughts. It was an active process of the mind which required some effort. In this sense, meditation was really undistracted concentration. When practised long enough it led on to:

3   Contemplation

In contemplation, the act of concentration became automatic and effortless. It was as if the mind slipped into overdrive. When this occurred, instead of the logical, thinking part of the mind being at work, the intuitive, creative aspect came into play.

It is important to recognise that the mind *does* have these two distinctive ways of functioning — one rational, the other abstract. Most of us are most familiar with the day-to-day rational processes of the brain. All day our brain is thinking, analysing, evaluating. We have a steady flow of thoughts from the time we first arise to the time when we lapse into sleep at night. This rational, mental activity is normally associated with the left half of the brain.

Normally, we would associate times of non-thinking with sleep or unconsciousness. However, we may have experienced fleeting moments of non-thinking consciousness in that pleasant reverie that sometimes descends just before sleep. This peace is similar to those wonderful moments when a glorious sunset or a major work of art touches our inner core and leaves us in rapturous silence. We are then involved with that more abstract, less rational brain activity which is associated with the right side of the brain.

Many of us, then, could be laughingly referred to as half-wits because, being rational creatures, we only use half our brain's potential! Contemplation is a way to exercise the other half. By doing so, fresh insights can be gained and new levels of meaning obtained. The mind, however, is still active during this phase of the process. In contemplation it is just being used in a way with which we are not normally familiar.

Prolonged contemplation leads on to a state of:

4 Unification

This is a still more abstract state. In it, the contemplater, the object of contemplation and even the act of contemplation merge so that there is no awareness of separation, just an abiding sense of unity. This union is what the mystics of all ages have sought so earnestly and waxed poetic about when they found. It led on to a final state of:

5 Illumination

This was described as 'the Knowing that passed all understanding'. In this state, totally new information would appear 'out of the blue'—the true revelation.

We can see how this five-step process works if we use the example of concentrating on a candle. Initially, concentration is required to sit still and to focus the attention on a candle. The mind may want to wander—What is for tea? What am I doing tomorrow? Should I scratch my nose? etc.

Eventually, with persistence and effort, we can concentrate on the candle without being interrupted by other thoughts. This is traditional meditation. Soon, it is as if another thought process begins and abstract thoughts of the candle become apparent. The symbolism of the candle, its shape, its light, its fire, may be reflected upon and their nature assumes a new level of understanding. This is contemplation. For example, you may feel as if the light of the candle is a symbol of the Divine Spark within yourself and feel enriched by this awareness. As time goes on such thoughts gently fade and all awareness of activity and time are lost. Only in retrospect can you be aware that you were in a state in which you felt at one with the candle. This is Unification. This sense of oneness may extend beyond the candle and your immediate environment to give a direct appreciation of your oneness with everything around you. This type of mystical experience puts a smile on people's lips that does not readily fade!

Finally, completely new information may come to your awareness with force and clarity. From contemplation of the candle you may have sensed the meaning of the Divine Spark; now, in Illumination, you may have direct Knowing that such a Divine Spark is within yourself and every one of your fellows. This Knowing is irrefutable. It is not the knowing gained through reading or listening to others. It is the Knowing of direct experience. It may not even be justifiable in rational terms; no worry, you Know it as Truth.

Health or Insight?

It is obvious from this example that an exercise which began as an exercise in developing concentration can lead into profound insight. This obviously is the basis of the active process involved in Insight Meditation and is quite different to the more passive, balancing, equalising Health Meditation.

However, the stillness of Health Meditation, the stillness obtained in our recommended version called Integral Meditation, is the same stillness described here as and experienced in the stage of Unification. The practical difference between Health Meditation and Insight Meditation is that the former begins by rapidly producing the Relaxation Response, so discharging stress and producing immediate Health benefits. Insight Meditation, on the other hand, can be quite an intense process, requiring concentration, perseverance and effort. In the early stages this can mean that there is a distinct lack of the Relaxation Response; in fact it can be accompanied by a sense of heightened arousal or stress. However, as we discussed in the early chapters, once any meditation technique is mastered, the peak experience is the same and all the benefits flow. The value of beginning with Health or Integral Meditation is the immediate and direct balancing effect and the subsequent health benefits.

This notwithstanding, if you have been practising the Integral Meditation technique and thoughts are frustrating you, you will not be calm and relaxed and you need something more.

This is where the use of a secondary focus comes in and, if used wisely, it will act as a stepping-stone into stillness. Let us get practical again:

Concentration techniques—stepping-stones to stillness

A   Sounds

For thousands of years, sounds have been a popular focus for concentration and meditation. The sounds can be internal or external in type.

(i)   Chanting

Repeating a sound or series of sounds aloud, externally, has always been highly regarded. It is pleasant to do, especially with a group, and frequently is a very effective way of being uplifted. Some Gregorian chants are famous, as are many of the Indian chants. Bhajans are a particular Indian form of singing that are like their counterparts, the Christian hymns.

Chanting is very popular at our residential programs with a favourite being:

> *Doors Opening, Doors Closing.*
> *Doors Closing, Doors I am Opening.*
> *I am Safe, it's only Change.*
> *I am Safe, it's only Change.*

This is sung repeatedly for ten minutes or so and is followed by a period of silence. It can be a very moving experience.

(ii)   Mantra

Using a mantra is the rhythmical repeating of a sound, a word, or a group of words, quietly in your mind, internally. In the Indian tradition in particular, the mantra has played a significant part in the guru, or teacher's relationship with his disciple or pupil. The guru was deemed capable of choosing the correct mantra to facilitate the pupil's safe and appropriately timed passage into the higher states of consciousness.

Transcendental Meditation (TM) was founded on this principle. The mantras used in TM are Sanskrit words. Beginners have their mantra specially selected by an experienced person and they are given instruction in how to repeat it. For many, especially those with an active mind, it is a useful device to control the thoughts. The idea is that one sits reasonably comfortably for twenty minutes twice a day. During this time the mantra is repeated and the passive approach is emphasised. If at any stage the student becomes aware of thinking of other things, then the mind is brought gently back to repeating the mantra. No anger, no disappointment, no 'Drat, I'm thinking of something else again'. Just leave off those thoughts and go back to repeating the mantra.

The mantra is a particularly good focus with which to set the process of meditation in motion.

Traditionally, the mantra is thought to be a word of power. Its repetition is believed to have particular significance and to be able to facilitate the process of entering deep meditation.

It is now well known that other sounds or words can be used. One group of 'heretic' Americans learned to meditate quite well using the words 'Coca Cola' as a mantra!

The types of mantras used then, can be classified into three main groups:

(a)   Nonsense mantras

These have no obvious meaning or relevance to relaxation or meditation. 'Coca Cola' would qualify quite well. Lawrence LeShan, in *'How to Meditate'*, described the 'LeShan Telephone Book Method' for designing mantras. He suggests opening the telephone book at random and taking the first syllable of the name that first catches your eye. Repeat the process to give a two-syllable mantra. He uses 'La-De' as a nonsense mantra.

This type of mantra does have the advantage of having no connotations or associations. It is therefore unlikely, of itself, to trigger thoughts.

(b)   Descriptive mantras

Letting go, Relax, Calm — all these are words that can be used as a mantra. They convey the intention of meditation and reinforce it, acting like an affirmation. Affirmations are short, precise summaries of intention that are used for self-programming towards a particular goal. So 'I am a positive person now', 'I respond with love now', 'I am worthy of love', are all useful affirmations which can easily double as mantras. One group member used the reassuring words, 'It will be all right' as a successful mantra.

(c) Spiritual mantras

These are the mantras thought to facilitate spiritual development and the attainment of higher states of consciousness. Some excellent examples are:

(I) Om Namah Shivaya

This is a traditional Indian mantra and is the main beginners' mantra used in the Siddha Yoga school. It can be used silently as a mantra and is particularly powerful when chanted with a group. I have found this a particularly powerful chant for beginners. If a large group is repeating it, it will often help bring about a breakthrough into deeper meditation. The words basically mean, 'I respect the divine within'.

(II) So Ham

This mantra is especially good to link with the breathing. Breathe easily, and mentally say *So* on the in-breath, *Ham* (pronounced Hummm. . .) on the out-breath. The sounds fit in very well with breathing and can be very effective.

(III) Christian Mantras

Be still and know that I am God is a longish Christian mantra, well loved and used by some, as also is *I am the Way, the Truth and the Light.*

Other Christian mantras are *Kyrie eleison* (Christ is risen) and *Hail Mary . . . Mother of God. . . .* There are many others and any prayer can also be used.

Just to repeat again, like any object of concentration, the mantra is to be seen as a tool, a stepping-stone to lead us into stillness. Its use does not suit everyone; for some it is a distraction at best, a downright irritation at worst. Like all tools, its work is done when we need it no more. While repeating it has its own benefits and using it will generally lead into a good experience of the Relaxation Response, there is more to be gained from moving beyond it, into stillness.

(iii)   Music

Music is another way in which sound can be used as a pathway into meditation. People have differing tastes. Some find structured classical works helpful; others find that this holds their attention and that they prefer gentle, lyrical, non-structured music. Either way, music can certainly be relaxing. However, it is often a challenge to 'let go' of the music and to move into real stillness.

Some people with busy minds have found that music, playing in the background at an almost inaudible level, helps them into successful meditation.

B   Thoughts

With this approach, the aim is to use the device of dwelling on one particular, chosen thought in an attempt to still the common flood of thoughts. A great benefit or side effect of the process is that, by practising it, major insights can be gained.

Various techniques have been used : Contemplation, Mindfulness, and the Koan. All belong to the realm of Insight or Analytical Meditation which will be elaborated upon in the next chapter.

Imagery is another process which can be used purely as a tool for Meditation or can be the basis of Creative Meditation. Here, too, we will explore imagery in more detail in the chapter on Creative Meditation. For the moment, however, it is useful to examine how imagery can be used as a secondary focus for our attention and so quieten those random thoughts and lead us into the simple stillness.

Imagery involves imagining pictures in your head. To do this, it is recommended that firstly, as usual, you relax. The eyes are closed and then most people 'see' the images as if they are on a TV or video screen in front of their eyelids. In my experience about three-quarters of an average group of people see images quite readily and clearly.

An easy exercise that will demonstrate it for you is to close your eyes and imagine you are at the beach. Take a moment to do it. What do you experience? Can you see it? How clearly? Also, did you feel it, smell it, hear it, taste it? The more complete the involvement of all the senses, the more effective the exercise will be.

If you have trouble seeing images like these and you feel you would like to, you can develop this skill also. Begin by looking at a scene or a picture. Really concentrate on it for about a minute, then close your eyes. You will probably see some form of after-image anyway, but try now to build up that same scene in your mind. With practice, you will find you can. Then practise building up images of scenes you know well, before finally moving on to creating fantasy images.

For the purpose of stilling the mind, there are any number of imagery sequences that can be used. All intend to hold the mind's attention, give it something to concentrate upon and, usually, to lead it by association into a calmer, more relaxed state. Ideally we then go on from there, into stillness.

As with all meditative exercises, it is best to begin with physical relaxation. Using the PMR exercise is ideal. If you can do it quickly and effectively without contracting the muscles, that is fine. Ideally, the more relaxed you are before you begin the imagery, the better.

However, if you are having trouble relaxing physically, being led through this type of exercise is another way of learning to relax. If you have the exercise on tape, or someone reads it out for you, slowly, deliberately and unemotionally, you will find it physically relaxes you as you go. If achieving physical relaxation has been a problem for you, sit in the prescribed position and simply concentrate directly on the imagery, leaving your body to relax as your mind does.

Many of these imagery sequences have other uses as well. So the Healing Journey, a sequence I use in our groups, has a powerful, if fairly subtle healing effect. This imagery exercise uses archetypal, Jungian derived images to transfer a positive healing message into the subconscious. It also frequently assists new members into a good experience of stillness.

The Healing Journey Imagery Exercise

This exercise is available on cassette tape — see list at the back of this book.

In this sequence we will be going on an imagined journey through the countryside. Images will be suggested and the aim is for you to build them up in your mind as if you are actually there. Not as if you are watching a video of yourself in the country, but imagining that you are actually there, seeing with your own eyes, and building up the other senses as fully as you can, hearing, feeling, smelling and tasting where you can. With practice you will be able to build up all these inner senses and have a rich experience. Again, be patient with this, there is no need to force it, just build it up with practice.

In the sequence, I will suggest a number of country scenes. You may find that this kindles images of places you know well. Remember that this is your experience, your fantasy. Your mind can very easily accommodate building up a sequence of images that involves countryside in widely separated parts of the country. Be prepared in advance to be flexible.

You may find that, instead, all the images are the product of fantasy and are not 'real' places you have been to. That, too, is fine. Remember again, it is your fantasy. We will come to a pool and the option is there to swim. If you prefer warm water and it is cold and wintry outside right now, set the thermostat in advance! Give yourself a comfortable experience! Similarly, walking through the grass, program it so that there are no prickles or other unwanted images. Note that if unwelcome images arise spontaneously, choosing to change the picture to a harmonious one may well be part of a subtle therapeutic change.

Now for the exercise:

The Healing Journey

First take up a position that is basically symmetrical and just a little uncomfortable. Then bring to mind the images as they are presented. Aim to see the images of the countryside as if you are really there, seeing it with your own eyes; feeling, hearing, smelling and tasting. The richer the images you can build, the better. And you will find that you get better at it, too, as you practise. At the end of the exercise you will be lying down in a comfortable, favourite place in nature. If after this you find your thoughts straying and being intrusive, return to the image of lying in this comfortable, peaceful place, and again allow its peace and serenity to settle all through you and feel yourself letting go.

Just let your eyes close gently . . . turn your thoughts inwards . . .

remember that this is a time for healing . . .

Feel your body relaxing . . . feel the muscles becoming soft and loose . . . feel the tension releasing . . . feel it all through the body . . . deeply . . . completely . . . more and more . . . deeper and deeper . . . letting go . . . feel it in the forehead particularly . . . feel the forehead smoothing out . . . feel it all through . . . more and more . . . deeper and deeper . . . letting go . . . feel your body warm and heavy . . . your weight settling down into your chair . . . more than relaxed . . . letting go . . . completely . . . deeply . . . letting go . . .

Now, in your mind's eye, imagine that you are in a beautiful field, in nature . . . as you walk across the field, feel the soft grass under foot . . . look around at the trees, and hear the wind gently blowing through the leaves . . . look up at the blue sky, see the occasional white cloud drifting by . . . and feel the sun, warmly shining down on your forehead . . . you might like to hear the birds . . . look around at the scene, and as you do, walk gently, peacefully forward . . . and, as you move forward, you come to a pool, a beautiful rock pool with a sandy bank . . . you move down on to the sand and feel your feet and toes in the sand . . . at the edge, you take your clothes off and leave them beside you . . . if you like to swim — swim; if you like to paddle — paddle . . . and moving through the water feel it refreshing, vital, against your skin . . . you might like to dive under the water . . . feel the freedom of the movement . . . you might like to throw some water up into the sunshine . . . see the sunlight sparkle in the drops . . . watch and hear the drops splash back into the pool . . . moving through the water, you look ahead and see a waterfall . . . you move towards it . . . you might like to pass under it . . . feel the water tumbling down on your shoulders, refreshing, invigorating, cleansing — the water feeling like it is passing right through you, washing away any old, tired energy . . . you feel refreshed and vital . . . passing behind the waterfall, you see what looks like a cave in the rock . . . it looks inviting, safe . . . you enter into it . . . you see what appears to be a tunnel . . . it is dark, going off into the distance but, again, it is inviting, and you move into it . . . it feels quite secure, comfortable . . . as you move in, you see a light, off in the distance . . . as you move down the tunnel, the light gets brighter — and brighter — and brighter . . . until you come out of the tunnel, into the full light of day, the sun shining down brightly, warming . . . before you, you see a green grotto surrounded by palms, ferns, luxurious green trees of all sorts . . . and in the middle a grassy cleared patch with a bench . . . and on the bench a towel and fresh clothes . . . you walk down the steps towards the grassy patch, and take up one of the towels . . . feel it soft and fresh against your skin . . . dry yourself . . . and put on the clean clothes . . . and then walk off, through the luxurious undergrowth, to come out in a forest of tall, majestic trees, straight trunks reaching up to the sky, a canopy of leaves overhead, and the sunlight filtering gently down . . . you walk forward . . . smell the smell of the trees, the rich mulch underfoot . . . you feel the soft leaves as you walk forward . . . you may like to pause, to lean up against one of the massive trees, to feel its energy and strength . . . passing through the forest, you re-emerge . . . back at the field, and there you find a special place, a place that is special to you, a place where you feel very secure, very much at peace . . . you find a soft spot . . . and lie down . . . and, as you do, a feeling of peace, tranquility, settles with you . . .

Feel your body relaxing, even more . . . any muscle tension draining away . . . you feel so relaxed, you feel as if you could just float up above the ground . . . all sounds fade away . . . you relax, just floating . . . completely still . . . completely at peace . . .

One of the features of this imagery sequence is that it takes you to a very comfortable, safe and natural place. By imagining yourself in that place, by imagining yourself lying down and relaxing completely, you add another stepping-stone in the relaxation process. For many people, doing this in the mind aids not only the physical relaxation but the mental relaxation also. If you find your thoughts wandering, or you become disturbed in any other way, you can return to the image of lying in the country, relaxing completely, and to that feeling of floating just above the ground.

There are two benefits here. The sequence of images in this Healing Journey conveys to the subconscious subtle images of healing, regeneration, freedom and renewal. At the same time it can lead easily and naturally into a deep state of physical and mental relaxation. It can be an effective stepping-stone into stillness.

Please note that if you find one section of this exercise particularly helpful, such as allowing the waterfall to flow through you, you can spend a much longer period of time concentrating upon it.

Relaxation by association

This process of relaxing by concentrating on images of relaxation, can be a powerful ally in meditation. Remembering that sequence of imagining being in your kitchen, a busy city street and the country, clearly demonstrated the effects the mind can have on our state of arousal or relaxation.

Think angry thoughts for a short while and you soon will be acting angry. Think of calm, relaxed, tranquil things or people and soon that too will be your state. This is another reason to make your place of regular meditation a tranquil, peaceful place. Using external images like photographs or paintings of country scenes adds to this process, as does reading inspiring, spiritually orientated books before you begin. Obviously watching a horror movie immediately before trying to meditate would make it something of a challenge to readily settle into being calm.

Other useful associations then, would be to think of people or groups that you have experienced in meditation. If you have been in a group and shared in the feeling of group meditation, bring that feeling back to mind as you begin your sessions at home.

Knowing that others are meditating in their homes at the same time you are helps build this feeling. Our groups have a special time at 7 a.m. Eastern Standard Time (Melbourne) when we all aim to think of each other and share in that feeling of meditation. Those who practise prayer, add to this time their prayers and it has become quite a special time.

Many people are also meditating from 12 noon to 1 p.m. and from 5 to 6 p.m. It is nice to know you have company.

Creative imagery

To complete this section, mention needs to be made of using creative, goal-orientated imagery. There are complete chapters to come on Creative Meditation and exercises will be given there. For the moment, suffice it to say that the White Light Imagery sequence is so powerful a healing exercise that it has been included in the Creative Meditation chapter. However, it is also a very powerful stepping-stone into stillness.

In summary then, imagery is a useful tool that you may or may not wish to use. If you feel attracted to it, practise it regularly and again view it as a tool, an aid, a stepping-stone — another possible way of benefiting by an internal exercise based on concentration; and another way of making the transition into stillness.

Let us now return to another major area suitable for focussing our thoughts and attention.

C   *Actions*

For some, the path is best begun by concentrating on actions.

(i)   Tai Chi

Tai Chi is a traditional Chinese technique with a definite sequence of dance-like movements. Practising it can develop good relaxation, although it takes much practice to move into deep meditation. When someone is practising Tai Chi well, you can feel something special in the air. Gayle has been studying it for some years now and, when she is doing it, it is as if there is a cocoon of stillness around her. This may sound a little vague or nebulous, but it is a definite, tangible feeling.

(ii)   Moving Meditations

Other traditional meditative actions worth mentioning in passing are Zen archery, the Japanese tea ceremony, and the dancing of the Sufi Whirling Dervishes.

(iii)   Breathing

More practically for our context, breathing has been widely used. There are simple methods using counting of the breath, and more complex methods using more involved breathing exercises.

Zazen

Observing the breath is the basis of Zazen, a form of Zen meditation. One sits, relaxes, becomes aware of the breath moving in and out, and counts the breaths as one exhales. One count for each out-breath, counting from one up to ten, and then beginning at one again. It sounds very easy, and it is easy for the first round or two. After that, it takes a good deal of concentration and practice. The instruction is to keep aware of the breathing, to count, and do nothing more. Focus on the breathing and the counting. Be aware of that completely, giving it one hundred percent attention. Some people find it easier to count up to four before they return to one again. Another way is to count continuously rather than in cycles. This involves starting at one each time you sit to meditate, and counting on up to a hundred, a thousand, whatever, at each session. This can lead to distracting personal competitions to see 'how far I got today', but it does suit some people.

Every way takes practice and is a good exercise in developing that quality of selective concentration called mindfulness. This technique will be elaborated upon further in the next chapter on Insight Meditation.

The science of breath

The Yogis have long been the masters of the science of breath. The best detailed reference for this approach is Ramacharaka's book, *The Hindu-Yogi Science of Breath* (1960). Pranayama is the branch of yoga devoted to breathing, and its study brings many rewards. It teaches the rewards of being aware of the need to breathe through the nose and of practising the complete breath. The diaphragm, the middle and upper chest, are all used to draw in a full breath, to increase the body's oxygen supply, to ensure the elimination of old air and to exercise the whole respiratory system.

Concentration on breathing

There are many methods for developing breath control, both as exercises and as means of entering meditation. These also are good exercises for developing mindfulness. Here are a few:

Watching the breath

Relax and become aware of your breathing. It does not matter whether it is fast or slow, just be aware if it is fast or slow. Now imagine that your centre of your awareness is at the tip of your nose. You are watching the breath moving by, going in and going out. You will probably find it easier to identify, or see the breath going one way or the other. Now settle to watching the breath as it moves out or moves in. Concentrate on that alone.

The point of stillness

Relax and again become aware of your breathing. It does not matter whether it is fast or slow, just be aware whether it is fast or slow. Now follow your breath as it comes in through your nostrils and moves down into your lungs. Watch it then as it moves out of the lungs. Follow this movement for a few cycles and then become aware that there is a point where the breath turns. As you breathe out, the breath stops for a moment, turns and moves back in. As you breathe in, the breath moves down until it stops for a moment, turns and moves out again. Take your attention to whichever turning point you feel most attracted to and hold your attention on that point.

Controlled breathing

Take your pulse and count it — rhythmically, one, two, three, etc., to get the pace of it. Now, using that pace of counting, breathe in for four counts, hold your breath for four, breathe out over four counts, hold for four, then breathe in again.

There may be any number of variations on this technique. Many people find it good to use connected breathing, that is, not to have a pause and, say, breathe in for six and out for six, continuously. You need to experiment a little and be careful not to hyperventilate and become lightheaded. Once you establish a good rhythm, you can do it easily and effortlessly and move on into a good stillness.

Another variation is to take a short breath in and count the out-breath — one, two, three etc. — drawing it out for as long as you can. Then another short in-breath followed by the long out-breath.

Another Zen approach is to use this type of breathing with its short in-breath and long out-breath and to just count — one or two or three, etc. — for each out-breath, up to ten, and then start again.

Relaxing with the out-breath

A very simple breathing exercise which is particularly useful at the start of a relaxation/meditation session is to take a deep breath in and to then release it with a pronounced sigh. As you do so, feel any tension being released from your body, your muscles becoming soft and loose.

This exercise is very similar to the natural use of the Relaxation Response. When we are feeling tense and want to release it, we often do it naturally by taking a deep breath in and sighing: **Whew!** It is a natural release mechanism so we can repeat the process consciously and use it as a good stress release, a natural prelude to meditation. As you continue, feel yourself becoming more relaxed with every out-breath.

D Objects

The final class of subjects to consider as a focus for concentration is that of objects. These can be external ones or parts of our own anatomy.

(i) External objects

The obvious implication here is that the process begins with the eyes open, staring at the chosen object. As with mantras, the object can be a nonsensical one like a spot on the wall or roof, one with a direct association like a tranquil scene, or a spiritual one like an icon, statue or cross.

(a) Open eye meditation

In Raja Yoga, beginners are taught to fix their gaze on their teacher, concentrating on the spot on the forehead just above the mid-point between the eyebrows. They encourage students to keep their eyes open while meditating and certainly this can be done so that you lose awareness of what your eyes are registering.

(b) Candle gazing (See positions for meditation, fig. 8.)

Another approach is to begin by fixing the gaze on a candle. If your mind or attention wanders, come back to concentrating on the candle. As you feel yourself relaxing, allow the eyelids to drop if and when they want to. You will then find that when they do there is an after-image, an image of the candle you can see although the eyes are now closed, which will fade gently over a few minutes. For some, this technique provides a gentle, reliable way into the stillness of meditation.

(ii) Internal objects

This is really a combination of reality and imagery.

(a) The tip of the nose

Here one sits and relaxes with the eyes closed. Then concentrate on the point at the tip of your nose. As I mentioned, this is how I began and with very little other information or instruction, but a fair deal of persistence, did get into some experience of meditation.

(b) The point between the eyes

After a while, I found myself more attracted to fixing my attention on the point midway between the eyes and a little up into the forehead. This is the location of the mystical third eye and is where many people feel their natural centre is. Think of it as the still small centre within, the seat or centre of your being wherein dwells all wisdom and love. Concentration upon this point can be a very powerful exercise leading you to have actual contact with your Inner Wisdom.

I find it very useful to add this to Integral Meditation. Once you are basically relaxed, hold your attention at this still, small centre — the point between the eyes.

(c) Colours

Concentrating on this area between the eyes can also lead to the spontaneous appearance of colours. Usually these colours have the intensity of iridescent colours. Often they take the shape of a ball or ellipse and seem to move either towards you or away. Unfortunately, trying to study them invariably leads to their disappearing as your intellectual mind is reactivated in the process. Relaxing and going with them, frequently leads to the movement slowing. Sometimes it can feel as if the colour is enveloping you like a cocoon and if this occurs and you go with it, then the transition into profound stillness can be made.

In my experience, about 25 per cent of deep meditators have seen these colours. If they appear for you, merely take them as a sign that you are making progress, but do not dwell on them. If you get caught up with looking at them, you may have a pleasant experience as they certainly are accompanied by a feeling of wellbeing, but you will be prevented from entering a deeper phase of the meditation.

It is under these conditions that some small percentage of people have visions. They too can be interesting and fun, but are also distractions. A Zen student arose from his meditation elated with having seen a vision of the Buddha. Excitedly he ran to his master to share his experience. 'Do not worry', was the master's advice. 'If you keep practising, it will go away.'!

Summary

Keep it simple.

In this chapter, we have discussed a wide range of optional meditation techniques. The best one for you is the simplest effective one.

Start with the Integral Meditation exercise. It is simple and effective. Practise it for at least four weeks. If you feel frustrated, then add or adopt the technique you feel most drawn to of all we have mentioned. Practise it for four weeks. Give it a chance. Be patient. Practise it often enough so that you can use it with skill. Enough so that you do not have to think of how to do it, but can just do it.

You may find that you are drawn to practising and developing skills with a number of techniques. This is what I have done over the years. So now I have a range of skills to draw on for different occasions.

Just like driving the car again. When the road is good and the car is in good condition, you can just get in and drive effortlessly, it flows so easily. If the road is rough and muddy, the car is old and worn, the journey requires special attention, special skills.

So for me, if all is going smoothly, I sit on the floor to meditate. Crossing my leg, I let my eyes drop, feel a wave of relaxation move down through my body and let my mind settle. Any outside disturbances or inner thoughts pass by like the white clouds drifting across a blue sky.

However, if I have been out working hard in the garden and my back is tired, I will lie down on the floor. Then I might spend a long time (sometimes even a whole hour) moving my attention through my body, relaxing, releasing tension and feeling the energy in it building up again.

When, as happens, I sit, relax easily but find the stream of thoughts passing by so rapidly that they are distracting, I might choose to still them with the aid of a mantra or concentrating on my breathing.

Occasionally I do imagery, although for me this is something I have only spent a lot of time on when intent on healing.

When I have a particular issue to sort out, a problem to solve or something creative to develop or write, I often sit and actively contemplate it. I dwell on that subject and actively seek inspiration or insight.

So there is a range of skills, a range of stepping-stones to use, depending on the circumstances or the need. It makes the whole process of meditation a rich and rewarding inner adventure.

The next phase to consider then is Insight Meditation.

Chapter Seven

INSIGHT MEDITATION : WHAT IS REAL?

Now is the time to add another dimension to the consideration of meditation. Time to explore the purpose, value and techniques of the second great pathway in meditation, Insight Meditation.

From all our discussions on Health Meditation, it should be obvious that the benefit of it is one of regaining balance, poise and equilibrium. By entering that simple state of stillness, we can let go of all manner of troubles, fears and anxieties. As we regain our balance, our natural, inner healer is released, and gently, powerfully, effectively, health is restored.

Again, it is clear that health here means far more than physical health, that this is a process which naturally balances and heals emotional, mental and spiritual needs.

But there is more to it than this. Health Meditation leads to balance, poise and equilibrium. If the emphasis of our meditation is to achieve the state of stillness that is the hallmark of Health Meditation, we will receive all these very real and worthwhile benefits. There is another step, however. The jewel in the lotus.

Remembering the traditional five stages of meditation, Concentration, Meditation, Contemplation, Unification, Illumination, the stillness of Health Meditation is like the fourth stage, Unification. With it comes a great sense of unity, oneness and harmony. This is a great delight and experiencing it fully for just a moment will affect the way you feel and the way you approach each and every minute of your life thereafter.

But this is an abstract, mystical type experience. It brings a *feeling* of what *Is*, what life is all about and what our part in it is. Can we go a step further and really *Know* what *Is*, what is real? Can we *Know* with the same certainty that we know the taste of a banana, having had that direct experience of eating and tasting it?

This goes far beyond guessing at what is real, beyond working it out logically through second-hand means like reading books or listening to experts. Can we really Know?

There is a wonderful story about a group of pygmies in the dark depths of the jungle. They happened across something new that they had never seen before. Because it was so dark and the jungle so dense, each one could only perceive a portion of this thing. Up one end of it, one felt something long, thick and wriggly, and thought it was a snake. Another, nearby, felt something else, long, thick and smooth, and thought it to be a spear. One of the group reached upwards and came across a wide, thin flapping object like a fan, while down at the other end a fellow found a solid round pillar and imagined a tree trunk. Further on, yet another thought that he felt a small, thin rope. Of course, all these bits were part of a whole elephant! They were feeling its trunk, tusk, ear, leg and tail, but they could not see the whole picture.

So what is the Truth in our lives? We all have some contact with it, some idea, some knowing, our own version of what is real, what is reality. But what is the whole picture? Can we Know it?

Obviously to do so, to see the whole picture, to have that insight (inner sight!) would be to satisfy our life quest. Some of us choose to deny or ignore those basic life questions – Who am I? Where am I going? What is the meaning of Life? – putting them off as too hard. However, there is a basic human need to seek the answers.

Almost everyone I have met who was dealing with a potentially fatal illness has become preoccupied with these questions.

For some people, the reaction to the question can be one of denial. Perhaps these people are overwhelmed by the task of finding out, think it too high a mountain to climb and find denial the only effective way at that time to deal with the stress and tension of not knowing.

What is it all about? The saddest words I ever heard were uttered as the last words of a despondent, dying man reflecting on his life: 'What was it all about?' he said. 'I didn't understand any of it.' If denial is the issue, fear is its bedfellow. With this combination comes apprehension, anxiety, disharmony.

Those who have sought and found the answers are the ones who radiate calm and inner strength. Of the cancer patients, they will be the ones who say the illness was well worthwhile. To discover this knowledge, to gain this insight, any price is worthwhile. How sad it is that so many people (I include myself here) need to be pushed to the brink before they attend to the real issues in life.

So what is there to be gained through this Insight?

> *The concept is that there is a fundamental Truth to life and that it can be experienced directly in a higher state of consciousness.*

This is the concept of Inner Wisdom and its attainment. Obviously, if there is a basic Truth with its associated Laws and we could know it all, we would have a natural frame of reference for our actions. We would know our place in the world, its meaning and its purpose. We could then be fully content with that place and confident of how to act and react at any given moment.

Is this possible? Obviously, like the taste of the banana, the only way you will ever be convinced is when you experience its reality for yourself.

People say they have experienced it.

Those who do, seem to have that special something in their lives, they appear free of fear and are marked by poise, contentment and fulfilment. They appear to demonstrate, to radiate, Inner Peace. Hence the smile that comes from deep down inside and the twinkle in the eye. This is the value of Peace of Mind.

So here is the exciting news:

> *For completeness, Meditation needs to go beyond simple stillness.*

There is another step, another stage, and the active path that leads to it is Insight Meditation.

Now we still need to keep all this in context. Let us not get confused. When we discussed the traditional five-step process of meditation, this extra step was disclosed and presented as Illumination. This can be experienced spontaneously, quite unsolicited or unheralded as a flash of profound Insight that flows on naturally out of that simple stillness. But it is less likely to occur if the motive for meditation is to simply enter stillness. If we use the more active techniques of Insight Meditation, we are more likely to experience these extra benefits, the culmination of what meditation has to offer.

Let me point out the dual benefits and limitations of the simple stillness achieved in good Health Meditation.

The stillness leads to balance, equilibrium, poise — balance, but not necessarily profound change of a fundamental nature. Sure, Health Meditation changes the impact of, and our response to, stress. It reliably does provide a sense of harmony and order which in turn provides a more balanced and poised approach to all aspects of our life. In this it is like an effective, natural drug. It removes the effects of the stresses, strains and excesses of living.

There is a good analogy. Imagine a glass of muddy water. If you keep stirring it up, what do you get? More muddy water. If, however, you just put it to one side, let it be still for a while, the mud settles and you are left with the clear water on top. Now, when we practise Health Meditation, the mud settles, and we do experience a wonderful degree of clarity.

But the mud is still there. If we stir the pot again, up it comes and we have murky water again. We must continually take time out to let things settle and stabilise. So Health Meditation can be like other drugs — quite addictive! We soon can come to experience and know the benefits of this stabilising Health Meditation. It can take us to heights of experience both internal and external that we only dreamed of before. But we must keep going back. We must keep doing it and repeating the dose to maintain the effect.

Now there is nothing inherently wrong with this. Continuing to meditate leaves us with plenty of effective clarity, plenty of clear water on top, but what of the mud? If we meditate in stillness long enough it gets gently washed away — I guess.

However, a moment of true deep Insight, of Illumination, sweeps it away in a single stroke. To really Know, is to be transformed; for to really Know is to experience a whole new dimension of clarity and perception of experience. It is as if we have been seeing through a series of veils all these years and now they are lifted and we see directly.

So this is the difference of the two approaches:

Health Meditation leads to poise, balance, equilibrium and harmony. Insight Meditation leads directly to transformation.

Now, would you believe, that even here, as with all else we have discussed, there are levels of experience and options as to how to approach, practise and experience the specific benefits of Insight? There are!

The nature of Insight Meditation

There are basically two aspects to Insight Meditation.

A   Mundane Insight

The word mundane is not used here in any derogatory sense. One whole branch of Insight Meditation is to do with the analysis, understanding and resolving of day-to-day situations and problems. This is an active process seeking to clarify issues to do with our day-to-day, mundane business and leads on to the establishment of a course of action which will enable us to be most efficient and effective.

This is an intensely practical process, one that successful people often do automatically and one from which anyone can benefit by developing and practising.

B   Illuminatory Insight

This is attainment of the direct Knowing we have been discussing. This leads to clarification and illumination of really major life questions.

The principles of Insight Meditation

This type of meditation is clearly an active process. It begins with mental analysis and is really based on a quest for understanding and truth. Like any quest, it can be exciting! It can easily lead to inner tension and arousal, therefore it is a very different process to passive Health Meditation.

Interestingly, scientific studies do show this difference. Maxwell Cade's 'Two-Correlated Graphs of Altered States of Consciousness' were first described in November 1974 to the Society for Psychomatic Research at the Royal College of Physicians in London. (See Appendix I for details.) The EEG and Basal Skin Resistance patterns of Zen meditators show the pattern of a relaxed body with an alert, active mind. Deep, simple Health Meditation, like deep sleep, however, is characterised by a relaxed body and a relaxed mind. Here again, evidence of this difference: Health Meditation is a state of profound physiological and psychological rest, Insight Meditation is an active state of inner enquiry.

This evidence adds reinforcement to the advisability of establishing a good practice of simple Health Meditation before embarking on other aspects of meditation. The Health Meditation ensures a balance, a good foundation from which to move off into new territory.

Now to complete this, it must be said that if you do plunge into the depths of Insight Meditation and find what you want, you are liable to undergo a complete transformation which will involve all the benefits of Health Meditation. You can reach the peak of the mountain using this route. Just be aware that the experience along this path is naturally different. It can take a long time to reach the peak — remember, twenty years in Zen meditation is not considered a long time.

It is possible that, while a good deal of progress will be made pursuing this path only, it may be a long time before the real benefits of balance are experienced.

It seems that there are many people who have pursued this path of Insight Meditation only, and who for many years have not found balance in their lives. Whether this is of a physical, emotional, mental or spiritual nature, it seems that imbalance can be of major significance to them and those around them.

Hence the recommendation to establish a good practice of Health Meditation first. Attend also to your diet, exercise, and other aspects of physical health, so that the balance is maintained and built upon.

As time goes on, if you do want to develop a practice of Insight Meditation, continue the passive Health Meditation independently of this more active process. Do sessions of each. Be sensitive to your needs. As you practise you will intuitively know what is required.

The two naturally complement each other.

Techniques of Insight Meditation

There are two main techniques or approaches to consider. While they overlap somewhat, both are very useful to be aware of and practise.

A Analysis: *To know what is*

This is the path of questioning, of seeking, analysing. The path of knowledge. To seek solutions to problems, to know what the answers are.

There are techniques for developing insight into mundane and major life issues and, as said before, it is a wonderfully practical, problem-solving device.

B Mindfulness: *To observe what is*

This is a more erudite path. It is to do with seeing what is, what is really happening in any given situation. This is the Path of Observation and aims to build an ability to perceive accurately.

So often what we perceive in our lives is coloured by past conditioning, past memories and associations, as well as concerns or preoccupations for the future. It is as if we are living out of time, beset by past and future.

The aim of mindfulness is to enable us to break free of the past and the future and to be here now. To respond openly, freely and fully to this moment right now; to respond appropriately to this moment right now; to give one hundred percent attention to everything we do, confident in the knowledge that we can do no more, that anything less is inadequate, and that when we do give one hundred percent attention to all we do, we will feel complete, satisfied and at peace.

So often it seems we have the attitude that if only that thing had not happened in the past, I could be different. If only I can put up with the way things are now, put up with what needs to be endured now, make the effort now, then things will be better in the future. If I suffer this unhappiness and sacrifice now, then with a bit of luck, hopefully things may be better soon. I will be happy in the future—one day. What a recipe for unhappiness! Not to mention stress.

However, giving attention to this moment, each and every moment, finding meaning, purpose and satisfaction in it, is a sure recipe for peace of mind.

It is helpful to dwell on the fact that right now, as you are reading this, you are at the pinnacle of all human evolution. All the history of the world, all the development of the Universe itself, is at its peak right now. You are it. State of the art human being!

Now, someone has gone to a great deal of trouble to set all this up. All that history, evolution, progress. And here we are, not only experiencing it, but adding to it. What a special place to be! What a privilege.

When we hold on to this sense of specialness in every moment, in the good times and the bad, then we can experience mindfulness and with it, profound satisfaction and peace.

It means also that the experience of reality we are having right now is the best we will ever have. What happened yesterday, no matter how good it was, is now just a somewhat faded product of our memory and all its limitations. That memory has nothing of the reality that this moment right now has. And as for the future, who knows? It would be nice to think we will all have full, long, healthy and productive lives, but who can guarantee even tomorrow? Again, our fantasies for the future have nothing of the reality of this moment we are experiencing right now. Especially if we experience it with mindfulness, giving it full, undiluted attention.

So how do we develop these two qualities of Analysis and Mindfulness?

Analytical Insight Meditation techniques

1   Contemplation

This technique is based on the traditional five-step process of meditation: Concentration, Meditation, Contemplation, Unification, Illumination.

(a)   Basic Contemplation

In this approach, the focus for concentration is one particular subject to think about. The aim is to think about that one thing and to exclude any other thoughts.

Begin these sessions by relaxing physically and mentally as much as possible. Practise the Relaxation Response. Then start the analysis. Keep concentrating on the topic; if your mind does wander, come back to the topic as soon as you realise you have lost it. Absorb yourself in the topic, ask yourself questions about it. Think of experiences you have had that relate to the topic, the pluses and the minuses, pursue it with rational, intellectual analysis, indulge in an internal debate.

Pursue the doubts and cynical thoughts that arise. They, too, are relevant, and understanding them will help clarify the issue. What are the facts and how do I feel about them?

Hold on to the thought like a terrier with a favourite bone. Then, if you have a moment where an intuitive insight unfolds, stop seeking and give full attention to the feeling of understanding you are experiencing. It is often like a window opening into a wider understanding, like seeing a broader picture. This may well leave you feeling that you now have a wider grasp or knowing about the subject.

During a session, when such a feeling of insight occurs and then fades, you can either return to more analysis, more contemplation, or finish the session. Often in this way, by returning to the same subject repeatedly, you can have a series of mundane, useful and practical insights in a lead-up to a more major Illuminating Insight.

This approach has been used widely in many cultures. Traditionally, Christian students of meditation were trained to contemplate an ideal such as Love, Truth, Justice. The idea was to think about anything to do with the subject and not to stray on to other topics. While the thoughts stay on the theme of, say, Love, you are being effective. If you find yourself getting off the track, come back to 'Love', and start again. This process can lead you into minor insights during the Contemplation stage. It may well lead on to a feeling of being at one with, or Unified with, the topic, in this case Love, and may even lead on to a major revelationary Insight about its deepest nature. This then is an Illuminating experience.

(b)   Insight via Structured Association

A good example of how to seek Insight in a structured way, is the Eastern meditation, 'The meditation of the thousand-petalled lotus'. This technique is used to examine a central theme, say for example, the nature of Love. One sits and relaxes, thinks of Love, and waits to see what associated thought arises.

The aim is to spend only three or four seconds on each association and to recognise whether or not there is a connection. You are not aiming for anything more. Just to identify the association and see whether or not you can connect the two. It might go like this: Choose Love as the centre of the lotus. The first thought might be 'mother'. Yes, can see the connection. Back to Love. 'Wife'. Yes, understand the connection. Back to Love. 'Children'. Yes – and so on. Then you might find that the thought 'enemy' arises, and that you do not understand it immediately. You say to yourself, No, and go back to the central theme and await the next association. As you persevere with the exercise you may get an insight via other associations as to why love and enemy could be associated.

This technique may sound simple, but with regular practice on any one given topic, it can lead to powerful insights.

A similar thought process can be used to think about, to contemplate, practical issues like what to do and how to solve specific problems. Anything can be chosen and used as the theme for the centre of the lotus. Used consistently it can lead to powerful insights as it leads on to the higher stages of meditation. One can use it to simply sit down and contemplate what is the best approach to take towards our eating habits, about what to do at work, or any other decisions we face.

(c)   Self Analysis

One particularly useful way to use this contemplative process is to dwell on basic life questions such as 'Who am I?' This can be a very powerful meditation leading to valuable insight. It can be used in a highly structured way by posing the question: 'Who am I?'

For example, you sit, relax and dwell on 'Who am I?' You may say, 'I am this body'. The reply is to say, 'Who is the I that is aware of this body? I know that if I lose a leg, I may lose one-quarter of my body, but I do not feel any less of a person. I still feel like "me". 'Who am I?' You may respond, 'I am these emotions I feel'. Then the reply is, 'No, emotions are something I feel, they come and go. Who is it that feels those emotions? Who am I?' You may then decide that, 'I am these thoughts, these memories, these attitudes'. The reply is, 'No, those thoughts are in my head, they too come and go. Who has them? Who is aware of them? Who am I?'

As you continue this process of elimination, of question and answer, you will find yourself coming back to a central core deep within your outer shell. It can well lead to great insight and again needs to be practised regularly for weeks or months for best effect. This constitutes meditation for personal discovery and development.

The Koan

A particularly Zen approach to stilling the mind, the Koan is a device intended to overload the rational way of thinking, so causing it to shut down altogether. This creates a space in which other aspects of the mind can function and insight can follow. The idea is to present a riddle-like question, to place great importance on the answer, but for there to be no definitive answer. Perhaps the best known Koan in the West is, 'What is the sound of one hand clapping?'

Often out of a Koan comes an insight into how the mind works. Here is a delightful example: Imagine that a man is keeping a duckling in a glass bottle. As he feeds it, it grows and gets stuck for space. The man wants to get his duck out, but he does not want to break the bottle. How can he do it?

One answer is: It is done!

The only person I have met who got an answer quickly was a six-year-old girl who was asked to help her grandfather solve it. She replied to him – rather caustically he confided – 'Granpa, if you are silly enough to imagine a duck in a bottle, I am sure you can imagine it out of the bottle'. It is all in the mind. It is done!

2   Mindfulness

This is particularly the way of Zen meditation but it is touched on by most other traditions. I have the impression that Zen has built up something of a reputation for being esoteric and impractical. However, this, in fact, is far from the truth. Zen is very practical. Zen is based on being here now, being aware of each and every moment and utilising it to the full.

Traditionally, young Zen students in Japan spent one or two years in full retreat in their monastery. There they were taught to concentrate and meditate. Their daily program emphasised the joy of hard physical work and of finding value in even the most mundane tasks.

Then, after this cloistered time, unless they had an overwhelming desire to become a monk for life, they were encouraged to return to the world, to have families, to join in commerce or wherever else their talents lay and to put their skills to practical use for the benefit of all. They possessed the ability to concentrate, to persevere, and to work hard. They also had a humble, optimistic life outlook and so were responsible for much good within their communities, frequently becoming civic or commercial leaders.

The method of Zen is simplicity itself. Learn to concentrate. To be aware of what is. To get free of unwanted distracting thoughts, to learn the art of selective concentration. To be mindful.

In Zen, mindfulness is taught, practised and experienced through breathing.

Zazen

This is the core of Zen. We have already touched on it and now, to elaborate, there are three important factors : position, breathing and attitude.

The position

The ideal position for Zazen practice is sitting in the Zen lotus position as described earlier. You may need to start cross-legged, or in half lotus; serious students of Zazen are encouraged to use the complete posture as soon as possible.

(Note again: For beginners this can be quite stressful, the pain can be quite an issue. While it is a calculated part of this exercise, it does not lend itself to achieving the benefits of the Relaxation Response and simple Health Meditation quickly.)

The breathing

Breathing should be diaphragmatic and of a particular nature.

When you breathe in, the tummy should go out; when you breathe out, the tummy should go in. This is diaphragmatic breathing. You should then take a short in-breath, followed by a long, extended out-breath. At first this may seem unnatural. As you practise, it will take up its own easy rhythm and the out-breath will become still longer.

Each time you breathe out, count One, then Two on the second out-breath, Three, etc., up to Ten. Then start again.

This is the traditional way. You may find it easier to only count to four to begin with.

The exercise is to keep aware of the breath and to keep counting.

The attitude

The attitude should be one of alert concentration. Imagine a prisoner with a full jar of oil balanced on his head. He is being led through a busy thoroughfare with a guard at his rear. The guard has a huge sharp sword and has been instructed that if one drop of oil is spilt, he is immediately to lop the prisoner's head off. The need for the prisoner to pay full attention to his balance, to being relaxed, to go with the movement, to not be distracted by the crowd around; that need, that concentration, is the concentration to take into Zazen.

Follow the breathing, be absorbed with it, give it full attention, do not waver. However, be prepared to be gentle with yourself when you do! Be prepared to come back again and again to the breathing and the counting.

When you start you may find you can only hold it for a minute or two. This exercise will teach you concentration, single-minded concentration, mindfulness.

The practical nature of mindfulness

When you are washing the dishes, how often are you concentrating upon washing the dishes? How often are you thinking of the day's past events or plans for tomorrow? How often, therefore, are you out of time? When you are doing that, when you are out of time, not paying attention, you are not really living, you are merely existing.

When you wash the dishes, washing the dishes must be the most important thing in your life. Mindfulness. That same degree of focussed attention.

A Zen master asked about the nature of Zen said, 'When I eat, I eat. When I sleep, I sleep'. Not eating in front of the TV and being stimulated or depressed by those images, but eating with full attention being given to the eating.

There is another wonderful Zen story of a monk walking through a forest. Suddenly he became aware of a tiger stalking him. Running through the jungle he came to a precipice, the tiger hot on his heels. Without hesitation he leapt over the edge and, sailing down through the air, was fortunate to become stuck on a small, gnarled tree growing from the side of the rocky cliff face. As he considered his position, perched on this tree, high above the forest below, he noticed the tiger's mate circling underneath him. With one tiger above, another below, his gaze settled on a wild strawberry growing out of the cliff face. How sweet it tasted!

This is a wonderful story of poise. Of responding to the moment, to the opportunity that presents. To not be paralysed with fear by what was behind or in front, but to see the beauty of the moment. To taste the full sweetness of the very special experience presented by that strawberry.

Sometimes people say, well, what about dealing with the past or planning for the future? When it comes time for planning, do planning. Sit down formally and give yourself one hundred percent to planning. Itineraries, meetings, timing etc., are all important parts of daily living. But make your plans, then leave them. No need to dwell on them. Do your planning, then respond to the moment, deal with what comes up. Be there when the meeting is on and really be there. Be with that meeting, do not be off in your mind planning some other jaunt.

This way every act of every day assumes significance. For me it is not unreasonable to say *sacred significance*. Planning, meetings, washing the dishes, eating, every moment of our lives should be precious or meaningful, given full attention as if it might be our last. Even suffering is ennobled when viewed in this way.

What more can we do? Anything less is not enough.

Part Two

ACTIVE MIND

Chapter Eight

THE ACTIVE MIND—TAMING THE TIGER

The still mind brings equilibrium. The analytical mind brings insight. What now of the active mind? With all the talk of the advantages of stillness, is that more dynamic, logical, rational, thinking mind nothing but a hindrance to our progress and happiness? Obviously not! Without it we could not function in this world we are experiencing. If we did not have a mind to work with, how would we survive, let alone remember or learn who we are and where we are going?

Everyone realises that the active mind has an enormous potential to guide and direct us. Clearly, however, it can destroy. It will influence everything we do as it interprets our world, both inner and outer, and leads us forward. As Henry Ford said:

> *"Whether you think you can,*
> *or you think you cannot,*
> *you are right!"*

Positive Thinking has its place, too

So now it is time to turn our attention towards understanding the function of the mind. We seek to understand what the active, conscious mind is capable of, and what its limitations are.

We will examine how the subconscious mind can so dramatically affect our behaviour through the influence of memory, beliefs and conditioned habits. We will see that we can learn how to change unwanted habits once we recognise and learn how to use that vast reservoir of potential, the power of the mind, in an exciting, creative way. The challenge through all this will be to keep a perspective on the role of Meditation and Inner Wisdom and how we can integrate and utilise all these aspects to best effect.

But first the good news:

We are all positive thinkers!

Just think of an everyday thing like going on a simple journey — going to an important meeting. It begins in our mind, it begins with our thoughts. There will almost certainly be words there, describing what we are planning — the address, who we are to see and the time we need to be there. In our mind is the goal. Perhaps we have a picture of it also. Having been there before, we can see an image of the building quite clearly. Or we have looked up a map to work out how to get there. Finally, there will be a feeling attached to going to the meeting, good or bad, and a commitment to be there.

So having established this clear goal, our mind then helps us make the appropriate choices to get us there on time. We may choose to go by car. If we get out to the garage only to find the car has a flat battery, will we abandon the goal? Unlikely. Almost certainly we will rally around, and do whatever it takes to get moving. Ask the neighbour for jumper leads, call a mechanic, push the car downhill to jump-start it — whatever it takes.

As we set off, we turn left or right onto the highway depending on the choices the mind makes in order to take us towards the chosen goal. If, when we are halfway along our chosen route, there is a bridge to cross and it is blocked by a major accident, will we abandon the goal? Probably not. It will seem very natural to back up and find another way around. We have done this so many times before, it seems so reasonable to complete that journey, to attend that meeting, why should we give up so easily? We keep going, making every effort to reach the goal.

This is positive thinking working naturally and effortlessly, but extremely powerfully, helping us to achieve reasonable and worthwhile goals in life. We all do it regularly in many different ways.

While we are all positive thinkers, then, it would seem fair to say that some are more positive than others! Getting to a meeting, getting ourselves home, that is easy. But when it comes to more complicated life situations like managing our children's welfare, managing a business or dealing with a major, life-threatening illness, not everyone it seems, applies these same simple, basic, and yet so powerful techniques.

In the health area, for instance, I am quite sure that there was a period in my life extending well over two years during which my health and my life were in the balance. There were many ups and downs during that time, many obstacles to overcome. I am sure that if at any stage during those two years I had lost that positive attitude, that determination to push on and to regain my health, if I had given up mentally, I would have gone under and not recovered.

I was fortunate to have had this positive attitude, and doubly fortunate to have it reinforced by my very positive wife. However, we also did a lot to develop and maintain this attitude. Like any life skill, people differ in their natural talents and start at different levels.

And now the second piece of good news:

Being positive can be an acquired skill!

We can identify the principles of positive thinking, add to this an understanding of how the mind works, and then apply this knowledge with wonderfully creative results.

Let us begin by returning to the essentials of positive thinking. There are three major principles:

1 The first principle of positive thinking

Develop a clear goal

If you did not know the address, if you did not know the time of the meeting, how could you possibly hope to get there? You must have a clear goal, a precise target to aim for.

2 The second principle of positive thinking

Having developed a clear goal, you must then:

Be prepared to do whatever it takes to achieve that goal

This is essential, a key to success in any area of human endeavour. When you have a clear goal, are committed to it and are prepared to push on towards it no matter what, you become extremely powerful and virtually unstoppable. You are assured of success.

3   The third principle of positive thinking

This is the trick that really makes it all work!

Choose to enjoy doing it!

How often do you hear people saying, 'I hate going to work but I have to', as if there was no choice in the matter. I always delight in saying, 'But you do not *have* to'.

'But there are the bills to pay, I need the money'.

'You don't *have* to pay the bills! There are heaps of people out there who are professional non-billpayers.'

'But I couldn't do that', comes the exasperated reply.

'Fine', I say. 'Neither could *I*! So *you* are doing what *you* need to do—going to work to pay the bills. *Why not enjoy it as well*?'

This question of choice is a key issue. Understanding that we do have a choice in all things brings us great freedom. As far as I can see, there is only one thing we *have* to do. It seems highly likely—in fact, all the evidence points to it—that we do have to do one thing: We almost certainly have to die one day. Everything else along the way, however, is a matter of choice.

'But I have to look after the kids'.

'Who says so? Some kids do get abandoned. We have a good welfare state. They get picked up and, while their lives may be severely affected, they usually survive. Is that what you want to do?'

Most people, like me, say, 'No, of course I couldn't do that'. Just seeing that you are exercising that choice brings great freedom.

'Well, you do *have* to eat', they say.

'Well, I don't!' I reply. 'If I do not eat, very likely I will find out about that one thing I *do* have to do eventually a little earlier, but it remains a choice!'

Appreciating the choice brings freedom. Choosing to enjoy what we choose to do brings happiness.

Recently a member of one of my cancer patient groups, with a smile on his face and a twinkle in his eye, said, 'What is the point of feeling this sick and being unhappy as well?' He had a remarkable perspective. Despite his adversity, he chose to be happy. To understand this better, let us now look at how the mind works.

The Function of the Conscious Mind

The mind is a goal-orientated,
decision-making tool

When we believe it is fair and reasonable to achieve a particular goal, say to be at a particular place and time for a particular meeting, the mind will help us by making the decisions and choices that give us the best chance of getting there.

The mind acts like an automatic pilot

If you were shooting an arrow at a target, you would pull back the bow, take aim and let the arrow fly. If, when halfway to the target, a strong wind blew up, the arrow would be swept off course and miss the target. An arrow has no self-righting mechanism. We are much better than that.

The mind is more like an automatic pilot. It locks on to a chosen target and heads towards it, making choices and decisions intended to get us there as accurately and efficiently as possible. While doing so, we collect feedback and adjust our course to suit. So, if we are daydreaming about what is on at the pictures and miss a turn-off on our way to the meeting, the mind will suddenly register, 'This is not right. I have to go back—turn left—turn right', or whatever it takes to get back on course and reach the goal.

The mind uses this same mechanism to overcome any obstacles in its path, to back up, to find a new way, a new path. The active mind has an extraordinary capacity for creative problem-solving.

At the same time, the mind can selectively lock out distractions. So, if we are halfway to our meeting and a thought pops into our head, 'What a lovely day to go to the pictures', then, instead of diverging from the meeting, the mind rejects that thought and re-establishes the chosen direction. The mind locks on to goals that it accepts and believes in and does all it can to reach them.

It is helpful, then, to know that there is a fundamental goal and that each one of us is programmed to do all that we can to achieve this same basic mental goal.

> *The mind's fundamental aim, or target,*
> *is to experience peace of mind.*

Nothing is more important to the mind than to experience peace — peace of mind. So what, then, is Peace of Mind?

What Produces Peace of Mind?

> *Peace of mind occurs when*
> *our actions match our beliefs.*

When our actions, our experience of the world and what is happening in it, coincide with our beliefs concerning what should be happening in that world, then we feel all is well, we are content, we experience Peace of Mind.

If we believe it is in our best interests to be at that meeting, we do everything possible to get there. To begin the journey at the appropriate time, to be doing all that is possible to reach its end, to be making good progress and, finally, to actually arrive at the destination — all stages of this process bring peace of mind. To be thwarted or frustrated at any stage would cause us to lose that sense of contentment and would produce a feeling that things are not right.

Doing what we believe in — acting in accordance with our beliefs — is a basic human need.

Obviously, what we believe in then, is very important. So, just what are beliefs?

The Crucial Role of Beliefs

> *Beliefs are what the mind*
> *accepts as being real.*

I had a friend in the Army Tank Corps. One of his mates had an extreme fear of snakes. Frequently they went on manoeuvres in Central Australia and everyone gave this man a very hard time, teasing him relentlessly about his fear. At the end of one camp, most of the men drank heavily while this chap went to sleep in his tent. Some of the others decided to play a practical joke on him. They obtained a piece of rubber hose, wet it, crept into his tent, laid it over his sleeping throat and wriggled it. The unfortunate man woke up with a start, took a short gasp and dropped dead due to a heart seizure! He believed that a snake was crawling across his throat. The fact that it was only a piece of wet rubber hose did not prevent his mind from having a devastating effect. He died because of his fear and because he believed he had a real snake crawling over his throat.

While this is a dramatic example, it does bring out another vital principle:

> *If we are to judge ourselves sane,*
> *we must act in accordance with our beliefs.*

There is nothing more frightening than believing ourselves to be going insane, so we do everything possible to avoid it. If we had a fear of snakes, went into the back garden, saw a long black object in the grass and judged it to be a poisonous snake, we would have to be crazy to go out there in bare feet and ignore it. We just could not do it. The fact that closer inspection may reveal it to be a length of garden hose, does not prevent it from having the same, initial effect that a real snake would have on our behaviour. If we perceive it to be a snake, and believe it to be a snake, then, if we are to feel sane, we must act as if it is a snake.

> *To act in accordance with our beliefs*
> *brings peace of mind.*

Again, doing what we believe in satisfies our basic need for peace of mind. So the mind does lock on to, or act in accordance with, what it believes in.

How Beliefs Develop

> *Our beliefs become the mind's goals.*

Where, then, do these all-important beliefs come from? When what we believe in can affect our direction in life so dramatically, it would be good to think that these beliefs were actually the truth, the best and most appropriate goals for us to aim for. How do we develop beliefs?

Beliefs are a product of the accumulation of experience.

This experience may be direct or second-hand.

Direct experience is what we have absorbed for ourselves. We have an experience which we take in with our five senses — we see, hear, smell, taste or feel it. Clearly, if we are to form an accurate belief concerning what is real, the accuracy of this perception is vital. This accuracy is limited, however, by our five senses and any instruments we use to enhance them. So, if our sight operated on a shorter wave length, we might have X-ray vision. If this were so, our version of reality, what we take to be real, would be very different. Instead of believing people were fleshy and pink, or golden, or chocolate-coloured in their appearance, we would believe in their appearance in skeleton form as the norm!

As pointed out in the case of the hose and the snake, the perception of what is real may or may not be correct, Thus, beliefs based on direct experience are not always accurate. Importantly, however, and to repeat again, if we believe something to be real, then for us it is real, and we must act as though it is.

Second-hand experience is what we glean from the teachers in our lives, the people who tell us this happened, or that this is the way it is, that this is what we can or cannot do. Teachers may be people, books, cassettes, films, etc. etc., anyone or anything we are prepared to give the authority to — to tell us what is real.

Once again, depending on the quality of the teacher, beliefs gained via second-hand experience may or may not be accurate.

At one time, everyone had the second-hand belief that the world was flat. No one had ever seen the edge or fallen off, but the belief was very strong and it prevented the discovery by Europeans of large areas of the world for a long time. Nowadays most of us have the second-hand belief that the world is round. We have been taught this is so, we have seen globes and satellite pictures. It seems a very reasonable belief. On the other hand, some people actually have a direct experience of the world being round. They have flown around it, or sailed around it, and for them there would be little doubt in that belief.

Both types of belief are effective in this practical example. There is now very little fear of 'falling off' when international jets head off around the world. Clearly, however, *what we believe in will dramatically affect our life experience.*

Imagine two little boys attending their first day at kindergarten. Little Johnny is really pleased to be there. He had an older brother who started two years ago and told him about all the wonderful things that they did. His mother has talked of it and prepared him well by building up a picture of what will happen. And here he is, today's the day. First thing, around comes the teacher with paper and crayons—drawing time. 'Oh boy', thinks Johnny, and off he goes, scribbling away to his heart's content, having a great time. The teacher comes up, sees him absorbed in what he is doing, looks at his scribble and manages to find a tree in the midst of it all. 'Johnny, what a lovely tree!' she says and gives him a pat on the back. Johnny puffs out his chest. 'Whacko!' he thinks. 'This is pretty good. I'll come again tomorrow!'

Now little Freddy, sitting at the next table, is not so keen. He is the oldest in his family, no one has talked about school much. He is a little suspicious about it all and really would much rather be at home with Mum. In fact, he had to be dragged into the classroom, kicking and screaming a bit. He is really not at all happy. When the paper and crayons came around, he picks up one of the crayons, slams it rather roughly onto the paper, makes a few lines and puts it down again. The teacher, continuing her rounds, sees Freddy's poor attempt and disinterest. 'Oh dear, Freddy, you don't like drawing much, eh? Not very good at it? Never mind. Come over here with the blocks. Perhaps you can do some building'.

Now, it does not take too much imagination to guess what happens next day. More drawing. Little Johnny thinks, 'Oh boy, this was good yesterday. Teacher said I could draw lovely trees and gave me a pat on the back. Let's get into it again'. Little Freddy? 'Oh no, not drawing again. Where are the blocks?'

Little Freddy may be a latent Picasso, but if these early experiences are reinforced—as they so often are—he may come to believe he is a useless artist and may never develop his potential. He will be conditioned into a false belief. Soon he will be saying to himself, 'I cannot draw'.

The mind's role in all this is crucial.

The mind and the importance of beliefs

- The mind stores past experience to produce our beliefs of what is real — 'the world is flat', 'I can draw', etc.
- We then have a basic urge to act in accordance with those beliefs.
- This means our mind targets on to actions to fulfil our beliefs.
- Depending on our accumulation of past experience and our current perception of what is real, our behaviour will result.
- If our beliefs are positive, we are likely to have a positive experience of life. If our beliefs are negative, we are likely to have a negative experience of life. If you think you can, or you think you cannot, you are right!

So if in their teenage years our heroes, John and Fred, are expected to do a complicated drawing for a class project, their reactions will be quite different. Presuming those experiences have been maintained and reinforced, John will approach the project with enthusiasm. If halfway through the drawing he sees it is not going too well, he will stand back and say, 'What's going wrong? This is not like me, I am good at drawing'. He will find it no problem to rub out what he has done, start again, and do whatever it takes to get it right. And he will enjoy it! Poor old Fred, however, will be halfway through his drawing, stand back and say, 'Oh hell, here we go again, another fine mess! Never could draw, anyway. Never liked it. When do we get back to building?'

John's attitude, 'That's not like me', and his willingness to get his drawing 'right', raise another key principle:

When our Outer Reality
(our actions or our experiences)
conflicts with our Inner Reality
(our beliefs)
inner tension is created
leading to the motivation and creativity to resolve the conflict.

Imagine that through the years you have built up the belief that gardens should be free of weeds. Now that is a very dangerous belief! You have to act in accordance with it! So if it's a fine weekend following a week of warm rain, you may go out into the backyard thinking of a game of golf. What hits you in the eye? The garden full of weeds! The mind instantly locks on to those beds full of young weeds. It stands out so forcefully — that is not the way it should be! There is an inner conflict between what you believe and what you perceive. Immediately you are motivated, you have to do something about it. So you become creative.

The Wonderful Power of the Creative Subconscious

In response to inner conflict, a part of your mind known as the creative subconscious is stimulated automatically to resolve the conflict. Let us summarise the steps:

1   Using the garden example: perhaps at an early age you went with your parents to visit your grandparents. They had a garden free of weeds, filled with flowers and shrubs which you were paraded around to view. There was a warm happy feeling in the air. It looked good, felt good. You had an experience of reality, took it in with your five senses, and registered it via your conscious mind.

2   This information was then stored in the subconscious as memory.

3   As the experience was repeated, memories accumulated. You naturally came to believe that weed-free gardens are nice places to be in and so now you believe that is how your garden should be. In this way you developed beliefs which have come to form your version of reality. Now you find yourself saying, 'Gardens should be free of weeds', 'I can draw' or 'I cannot draw', etc.

4   If then you perceive a conflict between what you believe should be happening, and what actually is happening, an immediate inner conflict is produced.

5   This inner conflict stimulates the Creative Subconscious to act and resolve the matter, restoring us to Peace of Mind.

This process can be represented diagrammatically:

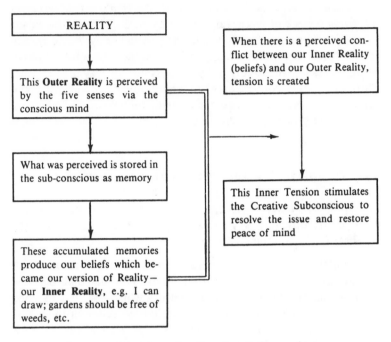

Steps to Stimulate the Creative Subconscious

The exciting thing about the Creative Subconscious is that it works on the subconscious level and so has free access to all our memories. As science knows, everything we have ever done, heard, seen, learned; every experience we have ever had, is retained and stored in our memory banks. But, as many of us know, getting access to it is not always so easy! Whether we just cannot recall it, or whether it is 'on the tip of our tongue', often we know we have the answer to a problem, but just cannot produce it.

All of us are certain to have experienced the marvellous Creative Subconscious at work. How often have you had a major problem, a real challenge, and you work away at it, analysing, thinking, reading, talking—there must be a solution, but what is it? In frustration you go to bed or go for a walk and then, at that magic moment when you wake up, or the sun just catches the trees – Pow! There is the answer, like a flash out of the blue. It is, in fact, neatly presented to you by that wonderful ally, the Creative Subconscious.

When activated by the Inner Tension that the problem has developed, that Creative Subconscious produces a powerful, natural motivation for resolution, and an extraordinary range of creativity.

So, back to the weeds in the garden. Fired by the conflict between belief and reality, you creatively seek a solution. You bribe the kids to pull them out, or you phone a gardener, or you do it yourself. If it is a warm sunny afternoon and there is nothing else you would choose to do, chances are it will be a pleasure to pull the weeds out yourself. If not, it may become a real chore. As we have discussed already, a challenge can be a constructive or destructive stress, depending on how we handle it.

However, if our life experience had been different, and as a result our belief concerning gardens and weeds was different, the whole challenge of weeding might not even have been there! If we believe that gardens full of weeds are fine, and that is the way our garden always is anyway, then no problem. Out the back door, there is the good old garden, full of weeds as usual. Everything's fine. Clear conscience, no conflict. Pick up the clubs, and off to golf!

So again, what we believe in will dramatically affect our experience of life.

Basic types of belief

There are three basic types of beliefs to be aware of:

1 *Casual Beliefs*

Casual beliefs are day-to-day practical beliefs: 'I believe it is going to rain tomorrow (based on what the weatherman said), therefore I believe I should take my umbrella with me to work'. These are short-term, practical beliefs, based on the balance of the available evidence. They are beliefs that do not matter too much. If we get it wrong, we get wet or we carry the umbrella around for a day unnecessarily, but no big deal. The mind is doing its useful practical goal-setting and decision-making, aiming to make life more efficient and enjoyable.

2   *Conditioned Beliefs*

These beliefs are of far more importance. Like little Johnny and Freddy—'I can draw', 'I cannot draw', 'I am good at this', 'I am bad at that'. 'It has always happened like that before, so now I expect it to happen again, and I will act in accordance with that expectation'.

These conditioned beliefs can dramatically limit our possibilities. In a recent football match, the team which had won the past two premierships and had not been beaten all year, was playing the bottom team. At half-time, the bottom team was in front! Imagine what was being said in the dressing rooms during that interval. The top team: 'What's wrong? This isn't like us. We don't get beaten by the bottom team!' The bottom team: 'What's wrong? This isn't like us. We don't beat the top team!'

After the break the two teams came out and play recommenced. This time they got it right!! The bottom team played terribly, the top team could not put a foot wrong—and won by twenty goals!

Whether you think you can, or you think you cannot, you are right!

3   *Core beliefs*

These are even more vital. What if you have had a lifetime of experience that leaves you feeling, 'I am a loser', or 'I am a winner'. These core beliefs, the answers to Who am I? What is life? and Where am I going?, will affect your whole approach to life and make a major impact upon your experience of it.

What is life to you? Is it safe to go out there, to take risks, to learn from your mistakes? Is life a rich and rewarding experience, a source of learning and fun? Or is it dangerous out there? 'Every time I try something, I get a slap in the face. It always goes wrong for me, why should I try'.

Obviously these basic attitudes will profoundly affect what you are prepared to go for, what goals you set and how far you are prepared to go to achieve them—and how much you enjoy the process.

So, being clear on what, in fact, you do believe in, is of vital importance. Most importantly, if you decide that you are unsatisfied with your beliefs, if they no longer meet your needs, there is a process available which will enable you to change them.

How to clarify what we believe in

A *Conditioned Beliefs*

To find out how you may be affected by conditioning:

(1) *Listen*

Really listen to what others say to you and also to what you say. Other people can show you an aspect of yourself you may not be aware of. Strive to be open to comment and constructive criticism, to view it objectively, and to say, 'Yes, that's right. That is something I need to work on', or 'No, that is their lack of perception. I am not like that at all'.

Most importantly, listen for your own key statements. How often do you hear people making self-defeating statements like, 'This is too good to be true', 'Something always goes wrong', or 'You can never find it when you want it, can you?'

If you make statements like that last one, you need to be very thorough. You need to hide everything very well! Because if you found it when you wanted it, you would think you were crazy, wouldn't you? I mean, you can never find it when you want to, can you? *Can you*???

What are those key statements? They will reflect your basic beliefs, and are so important because you will have a deep commitment to act in accordance with them.

(2) Observe

Watch what you do. Become aware of your patterns of behaviour, your habits, how you react in given, repeated situations. This, too, will give you a good guide to your inner beliefs.

Observe, too, what stands out to you, particularly what you see in others. The mind locks on to what it believes in and, commonly, when a major issue is active in your life, it will stand out in others. So, if you find yourself constantly coming into contact with people who are rude and insensitive, explore your own position in this regard and examine whether there is some work for you to do on that area.

Commonly, the people we meet day-to-day come to us as teachers. Like mirrors, they hold up aspects of our selves for consideration, development and resolution. We see in them what is important for us. Being aware of this can make personal development into a constructive, conscious process.

B   *Core beliefs and Insight Meditation*

We have already discussed the value of quiet self-analysis through inner examination. This is a wonderful technique and the most reliable way of all to gain insight into our true nature and what is real.

What are your core beliefs?

This is the process of self-analysis as described in Chapter Seven. The object is to seek answers to the three basic questions and complete these statements:

1   I am . . .

2   Life is . . .

3   My purpose in life is . . .

Clarifying these questions, or at least working on them and feeling confident that you are making progress towards an insight into them, is a basic requirement if we are to be happy and to experience peace of mind.

Having now gained some understanding of the way the mind works, let us go on to investigate how we can use this knowledge — how to use the power of the mind.

Chapter Nine

CREATIVE MEDITATION: USING THE POWER OF THE MIND

The mind has an extraordinary power to create or destroy. Perhaps one of the most convincing and extreme examples of its destructive power lies in the pointing of the bone in the Australian Aboriginal culture.

Pointing the bone

Now if an ordinary white Australian came up to you in the street, pointed an old bone at you and said you were going to die, you would probably laugh, think he had suffered an overdose of fried chicken, and go on your way. If, however, a tribal Aborigine did the same thing, using a human bone decorated with feathers, you might get just a little nervous. And if you were a tribal Aborigine yourself, you might be in big trouble for then you could well have a belief system that was based on the unity and cohesion of the tribe. You would be aware of the strict codes of conduct to protect and ensure the welfare of the tribe, and know that some of these codes were inviolable. If you broke one of these major laws, you would know that it was unacceptable for you to remain a member of the tribe. In fact, the accepted thing would be that you should die. The way you would die would be through the ceremonial pointing of the bone. So in that situation, to be confronted by a tribal elder and 'pointed', would have a dramatic effect. You would probably die in just a few days.

Interestingly, the other members of the tribe would react strongly also. The same belief system would also affect their behaviour in drastic fashion. Initially they would all withdraw from you, treating you like a pariah, an untouchable. Then, after you had withdrawn from life, had refused to eat or drink and rapidly had declined, they would, as you approached the end, all gather around again. Now you would be subjected to a display of formal pre-mourning, to reinforce the expectation that you were about to die. Death would soon follow with no physical explanation for how it happened. It would be the result of a powerfully activated belief system.

There are compelling reasons to compare this phenomenon of pointing the bone and the current-day diagnosis of a major, potentially fatal illness such as cancer. For here, too, there is a powerful community belief that cancer is a fatal illness. Despite the fact that 50 per cent of patients diagnosed with cancer do recover, and despite campaigns which aim to convince us that 'cancer is a word, not a sentence', many people are not convinced. Add to this the power of the authority involved here, the doctor, and the similarities are striking.

A person with a few vague symptoms, and perhaps a fair degree of apprehension, goes in for diagnostic tests. Then a man dressed up in a white coat, clutching a clipboard and with a stethoscope hanging around his neck (the symbols of office) calls him into an office. The ritual is frighteningly similar to that of the bone pointer. 'By the power invested in me as a doctor, I pronounce you a cancer patient who will die in three months' time. There is nothing that can be done to save you.'

Needless to say, the effect is electric. A reasonably healthy person is suddenly rendered non-functional by fear. Pain soars, appetites fail, work ceases, mobility grinds to a halt. The community does its bit. The patient is avoided where possible. Crossing the street to avoid contact, talking in whispers, smiling nervously as if everything is all right — all become effective ways of conveying the expectation that it is only a matter of time.

Faced with this 'reality', many patients become extremely punctual. As 'the inevitable' approaches, suddenly all the relatives and friends congregate to bid their last farewells, and thus, unwittingly, through this pre-mourning grief ritual, reinforce the expectations.

Now the above is an extreme view, but I challenge anyone to say it does not happen — often! Happily, the good doctors are learning, or have always known, how to convey major news. For cancer, breaking news of a diagnosis in words such as, 'You have a life-threatening illness and your long-term chances of survival are not good', leaves the way open for the patient either to leave it at that or to respond by asking for more details. Thus a statistical estimate like I was originally given leaves the way open for hope. I was told I had a five per cent chance of being alive five years after my surgery. My mind found it no problem at all to lock on to that five per cent and lock out the ninety-five per cent.

When things look even worse, there are still creative ways of presenting the facts without pointing the bone. I have contact with a surgeon who regularly is faced with this situation. When asked, he will be quite direct. He will say to the patient that there is no physical, medical solution for their situation, but that they are not limited only to that. As a human being they have other very powerful resources — they have emotions, a mind and a spirit, and amazing things can be achieved by mobilising these resources. People have recovered from apparently hopeless situations. He talks of examples he knows. He explains how some people have come to value other aspects of their lives over and above its length. His enthusiasm for approaching the situation positively is widely and well received. People feel better for having seen him and approach their situation with hope. Many take up the task of developing their own very real personal resources; many outlive their expected prognosis. Many, including the families, gain tremendously through the experience. A great number find peace of mind. Some achieve remarkable, unpredicted recoveries.

The placebo response

Of course, also on the positive side, there is the well-documented placebo effect. When a patient really believes that a treatment is going to work, it often will. This can occur despite the treatment being no more than a sugar-coated pill or an injection of water. There are numerous documented cases of pain control being induced as efficiently with well administered placebos as with genuine narcotics. Placebos are known to produce many positive results, in a wide range of illnesses.

The question remains: Do we have to rely on being tricked by a placebo, by what someone else tells us is real, or can we use this power of the mind consciously, through our own choosing?

Clearly we can. Once we understand how the mind works and can activate it, we can achieve extraordinary results. The last chapter gave us the clues. Now let's apply them.

To summarise:

- When we believe in our goals, they become targets for our actions.
- We must act in accordance with our beliefs if we are to judge ourselves sane.
- We therefore lock on to our beliefs like an automatic pilot, and lock out distractions.
- We are motivated creatively to achieve our goals/beliefs.
- We use feedback to determine our progress and then make modifications.
- In effect, we target ourselves to achieve the goals we believe in.

So with going to a meeting, we need to know clearly where and when it is to be held. If we commit ourselves to it, we are then motivated to be there and will be quite creative in making sure we get there on time. However, there is more to it than that.

Just having the goal does not ensure the result

We still have to get in the car and make the journey. There may be many steps involved and many obstacles to overcome. It is not enough to fix the goal in the mind and expect it all to happen, we have to make the journey. But one thing we can be sure of in all this is that if we do not have the goal, we will never begin.

Interestingly, probably more people die in their cars attempting to get to meetings than ever die of something like cancer. Yet few people baulk at the start of a car trip, paralysed by a fear of not reaching the other end. It is a sad fact that many do not make it, but we all seem to accept that risk quite readily. I suspect that with something more complex and uncertain, like aiming for the goal of recovering from a major illness like cancer, many people do hold back. They say, 'What if I fail? What if I do not achieve it?'

If success in a major illness is marked by death or recovery, if that is the measure of success or failure, it is indeed a risky business. On the other hand, if the goal is to live well, to take such a major life challenge as an opportunity to test your resources and to learn and grow, then the measure of success will be quite different. Physical progress still will be of importance, but there will be other issues like relationships, attitudes, spiritual values — real quality of life issues.

So again, to use the power of the mind creatively, we must have a clear goal. Once we have that clear goal our mind will do everything possible to help us to achieve it. Knowing all this enables us to use the power of the mind consciously, in an exciting creative way.

How to use the power of the mind

Here then is a summary of how it works:

1 Establish a clear goal.
2 Imprint that goal on to the Sub-Conscious so that it becomes a belief — a target for the mind to aim for and move towards.
3 This activates the Creative Sub-Conscious. The Creative Sub-Conscious then activates all our inner resources, giving us natural motivation and creativity.
4 This will lead to creative solutions and the impetus to carry through and achieve the chosen goal.
5 If we are smart, we will choose to enjoy the ride!

Let's now take a practical look at that initial first step:

How to set goals

This, the first step, is also the hardest. What should we aim for? To go with the flow and take what comes? To set tight goals in every avenue of our lives? Or some balance in between? What should we aim for? And who will decide what those goals should be? Can we work it out for ourselves? Can we decide what sort of meditation to do, and how often? Can we decide what we should eat? What sort of job to apply for? What sort of treatment to have? Or should someone else do it for us?

Who holds the authority for setting your goals?

Basically, is the person who decides your goals — those things that you can and cannot do — an external authority figure? Or yourself?

External authorities

Do you want to be told what to do? Do you want someone outside to take the responsibility for you and say, 'This is what you should do'? If so, whom can you trust?

This question of trust, for example, recurs as an issue of major concern to many cancer patients. I am sure it is a major concern for anyone seeking help to make any decision. You will only trust someone you know is well qualified for the task and with whom you can communicate and establish a working rapport. Qualifications are easy to check out and their relevance varies according to situations and needs.

The question of communication is a vital one, particularly in health matters. The great majority of doctor/patient problems I see are the result of poor communication. Basically, the issues are usually the consequences of *not* listening — really listening — in an open, active way. This leads to the doctor being unaware of the patient's needs or disregarding them anyway. Sometimes it is a question of patients not expressing their needs, or not being assertive enough to get those needs across to the doctor.

As a result of this, I strongly recommend that patients take notes in doctors' rooms. Certainly go in with a list of the questions you want answered; if necessary arrange for a longer consultation to handle them all. Some people take in tape recorders so that they can concentrate on the interview and check later to make sure they have not missed anything. I welcome this. It is intimidating only to doctors who are insecure, confused or under-confident. For patients and their families it is a very practical measure.

Still, the best working arrangement in any decision-making process is a partnership, with you at the helm. So, do not go to your authority figure and say, 'Here is the problem. You fix it. If you like, let me know how you are going to do it.' It is far more satisfying to approach it by saying: 'Here is the problem. How can we work on it together? How can you help? Make some observations and recommendations, please, and then allow me to decide my course of action.'

Internal authority

So, if you want to retain the responsibility, to make decisions and set goals for yourself, how do you do it? Do you guess? Or do you say, 'Well, I suppose this will do. Let's hope for the best'?

Surely there has to be a better way.

Normally when we are making decisions, we rely on two aspects of the mind — the intellect and the intuition. Both are important; both have their role.

Using the intellect to set goals

This is a matter of giving due consideration to all the options and then choosing the best one.

It is useful here to consider ducks. Yes, ducks! Ducks are delightful creatures, gentle and inoffensive. They always look as if they have some personal, inner secret that results in a supercilious smile curling around their beaks.

Ducks have great character — but unfortunately, few brains! It is simple to stop a duck — a low fence will do it easily. If you put a duck's dinner on one side of a low fence and the duck on the other, the duck will see its dinner and head straight for it. Bang! Straight into the fence! It backs off, shaking its head. 'What was that? Hmm. Now where was I? Oh yes, food time.' Straight for the dinner again. Bang! Into the fence, again, and again, and again!

If you think like a duck you will soon end up with a sore head!

A dog, on the other hand, has no such problem. Dog on one side of the fence, dinner on the other. The dog does not even bother to hit its head once. It will look to see if it can jump over, dig under, find its way through or around. It is good at looking for options, at being a lateral or creative thinker.

Some people call duck-thinking 'tunnel vision'. Interestingly, the more specialised we become in any field of endeavour, the more frequently tunnel vision seems to occur. Often we need to remind ourselves of the need to stand back and look for other options.

A surgeon friend of mine told me this story. The good doctor had been working late at his hospital one night. When he came down to the car park he found a man crawling round on his hands and knees under a street light. On enquiring, he was told that the man had lost his car keys and was looking for them under the light. The surgeon offered to help and he too got down to search. After some time the keys had still not been found.

My friend asked, 'Are you sure you dropped them here, under the light? They don't seem to be here.'

Oh no', replied the man, 'I dropped them over there, but it's too dark over there, this is where the light is!'

It is amazing how long we sometimes will keep looking for an answer in a place where it is not to be found. Thinking like a duck.

Before making a decision and setting a goal, we need to cultivate the practice of being open-minded – to actively seek out the other possible options, the alternatives, the better way, the best way. So it is good to read books, to listen to authorities, to talk, analyse, discuss, debate, and to seek information, guidance and assistance wherever we can.

When using this intellectual faculty, our thinking mind, it is an excellent idea to make lists. Say you are considering reviewing or changing your diet. There are so many options, so many authorities, so many seemingly worthwhile yet different alternatives. Which to choose? How to do it?

Make a list. List in detail the options the different authorities recommend – what to eat, what not to eat, how to prepare it all. Then make your own list. With food you can be quite precise. We will eat potatoes only with their skins on, we will bake or steam them, etc.

Without such a list, every meal can be a nightmare of confusion: Can we eat this? Can we eat that? Can we cook it like this or like that? However, once you have a precise list, you have defined the boundaries of what is possible and your Creative Subconscious can get to work. It can now come up with creative ideas on how to prepare that food so that it looks and tastes great. You still may choose to review your list periodically, to reassess it and make adjustments, but without that clarity at each step it will be a disaster. Once you have the clarity, everything will soon begin to flow and be enjoyable.

Using intuition to set goals

Some people are naturally intuitive and have a good 'feel' for things. On the other hand, what some people take to be intuitive guidance can be positively dangerous. It may just be wishful thinking! However, whether or not this inner direction works well for you, most of us are very responsive to it. Our decisions – our goals – need to 'feel right', as well as being intellectually sound.

This quality of intuition can also be developed into a valuable and reliable asset. The techniques are contained in the process of Insight

Meditation, especially in the phase of Contemplation. Out of the regular practice of Contemplation can come reliable insight and intuitive understanding of the nature of specific problems and their solutions. It is an extremely valuable tool and we have discussed it in detail in Chapter Seven.

Sometimes the process of Contemplation will lead on to an experience of Illumination. If this happens, any doubts or reservations will be removed entirely. You will know with complete confidence that you have made the right choice and set the correct goal.

On a more mundane level, it is to be hoped that any intuitive insight you may gain can be checked and validated with your own intellectual analysis. If you feel intuitively that you have made the right choice, and can justify it intellectually, you will feel very confident. You will have a strong belief in your choice and it will become an effective goal for you to work towards.

Goals to set

Remember first the major goals. What is your real life purpose, the essence of what you are doing here in this life:

My purpose in life is ---------

Then consider the broad picture of the many different areas of your life:

> *Your personal needs*
> *The needs of of your partner, marriage, family*
> *Your physical and mental health*
> *Your social life*
> *Your work or vocation*
> *Your education, recreation, creativity*
> *Your service activities*
> *Your retirement plans*
> *Your financial needs*
> *Your spiritual life*

Balance seems to work best. Go for it!

Now we come to the exciting part. As we have repeated already:

The Key to the Power of the Mind

*Believing in a goal leads to
all our inner resources being mobilised in a
maximum effort to achieve that goal.*

Now the startling and powerful fact that liberates the power of the mind:

*We can choose to believe
in whatever goals we consider important*

The beliefs we are holding right now are the product of accumulated past experience. Those experiences are stored in our Subconscious mind in the form of words, pictures and feelings, and our mind is committed to act in accordance with them. If now, we choose to set a new goal and want our mind to help us to achieve it, then the way to do it, is to imprint that new goal upon our Subconscious. By so imprinting the new goal, we will establish it as a belief. As we have shown, the mind will be committed then to acting in accordance with this belief. It will do everything possible to make the right choices, to give us the drive and motivation, plus the creativity, to find a way to achieve that goal. The mind will be locked on to the chosen goal and doing all it can to reach it.

So how can we establish a goal at this subconscious level, in a way that the creative power of the mind will accept it, work on it and achieve it? How can we develop new beliefs?

The imprinting process

We can choose to establish a new goal, to establish it as a belief that the Creative Subconscious mind will respond to, by using three components:

1   *Words*—or *Affirmations*, as they are called;
2   *Pictures*—or *Imagery*; and
3   *Feelings*.

Using these three components in the imprinting process is a big part of Creative Meditation. Before considering the techniques in practice, let us examine the general principles of their use.

The scope of Creative Meditation

Using Creative Meditation and the Imprinting Process is a very effective way to utilise the Power of the Mind:

1 To achieve chosen goals;
2 To change unwanted habits;
3 To create positive emotions, release unwanted feelings, and heal relationships.

One at a time, then.

1 Achieving chosen goals

Any goal that we believe in will act as a target for our mind. Once that goal is accepted as valid, all our inner resources, our motivation and creativity, will be stimulated to achieve that goal.

Any goal that we can establish as clearly as our expectation of getting to that meeting on time, will mobilise those inner resources and lead to a natural, maximum effort to achieve that goal.

With some goals, this will come easily – with others, it will be an effort. When we set a goal that can only be achieved far off in the future, we obviously start with both hope and doubt, like the positive and negative forces. Hope is *real* hope when we are both motivated to achieve the goal and have some expectation that it is possible to achieve. Doubt is when we are unsure. The stronger the conviction that we will achieve the end result, the more powerful the motivation and creativity that will be operating.

We can build hope, build conviction, increase our belief in achieving a given goal, by imprinting that goal on to our Subconscious. Again, this is done by using the techniques of Creative Meditation, the repetition of Affirmations, and Imagery, in association with appropriate Feelings. The imprinting process involves the repetition of the goal so that its claims to validity and reality are strengthened within our Subconscious.

Remember that the Subconscious with its memory banks is like a big, powerful computer. It stores all incoming information, sorts it and has it available for future use. However, it has no power of discrimination. It cannot distinguish between a real-life experience and one that we ourselves choose to feed in. So, if we keep telling the Subconscious that we can draw well by using an Affirmation, and if we add Imagery sequences of being able to draw, and a feeling of pride and enjoyment in being able to draw, we will soon have the Subconscious believing that we can in fact draw well.

Now, if we have had little Freddy's past experience of being unable to draw and suddenly impose this new belief, what will happen? If we do it thoroughly, we will set up a creative tension. Our new belief says we can draw; our experience is that we cannot. We have no peace of mind. We must do something to resolve the conflict or feel as if we are crazy. So we become naturally motivated and start to practise enthusiastically, read books on how to draw, attend classes etc., doing whatever it takes to fulfil the belief, the goal. At the same time we are bound to enjoy this new pursuit. This is the way to utilise the power of the mind.

This power is extremely potent. We can activate it in any area of our life that we choose. Setting specific goals in every area of our life is worthwhile as it gives our mind a target to aim for and it therefore naturally stimulates motivation and creativity.

Revise your reading of the section on goal-setting given earlier in this chapter and give consideration to Immediate, Medium, and Long-term Goals. Again, the greater the clarity in your goal-setting, the easier it is to imprint goals, to commit yourself to them, to enjoy them and to achieve them.

The goals might be very specific in terms of tasks to complete for this day, this week, this month, this year, this lifetime. Gayle and I like to sit down every six months and make a list of such things. We consider our personal, family and community goals. Then we refer to the lists from time to time, checking on progress, re-stimulating that inner process.

2 Changing unwanted habits

Ever wondered why New Year's Resolutions seem to make a habit of not sticking? How, despite the good intentions, the earnest resolve, they last only a few days and then the old habits resurface?

Most of us have habits we would rather be without. Perhaps it is something obvious like smoking. Perhaps we just want to establish a new routine of exercise or meditation. Many people attempt to change their habits through fear. Someone close, a smoker friend, dies of lung cancer. Someone else has a heart attack and pricks an over-weight conscience. We read of all the health problems associated with the average Western Diet and decide we really do need to change.

Fired by the fear, out go the cigarettes, on go the joggers, and major changes occur in the pantry. Instantly we create a new experience, a new outer picture—smokes no, jogging yes, and a whole new larder stocked with exotic 'health foods.' What happens? Frequently, the inner picture has not changed. The inner picture, the personal belief remains: 'I am a smoker. I do not jog. I eat and enjoy junk food'. So now there is conflict, an outer experience of no cigarettes, jogging and natural wholefoods, and an inner belief which is just the opposite! This conflict creates the motivation and creativity to get back to the inner picture, for peace of mind's sake.

This leads people to become very creative. At parties there seem to be so many people smoking: 'We are passive smoking anyway, so I might as well light up. One won't hurt.' Jogging? 'Well—Can't go out in the rain today. Don't want to be tired for that special meeting tomorrow.' Excuses and justification are easy to come by for a well-motivated Creative Subconscious! As for the food, every time you go to the cupboards, open them and look in, you reel back in horror. 'What's all this strange stuff doing in my cupboards? I must be crazy, where are all the junk foods?' So, again, you get creative. You stay out late enough on Sunday afternoon to be coming home late enough to say, 'Pretty late to be getting home; feel a bit tired; can't be bothered cooking tea. Let's just duck in and get a take-away—one won't hurt'. Then, next day: 'Well, we had one last night. It tasted so good, felt just right. Come on, let's go again', and again—and soon back to the old pattern.

The way our past life experiences have been built to create our beliefs or inner pictures, and making a sudden external change without an accompanying inner change, can be represented diagramatically:

Here, in the column on the left-hand side of the above diagram, is represented the accumulation of life experiences which, stored via our memory, produce our beliefs or our own inner pictures of what is real, who we are, what we can do, what the world is like, etc. If then, through fear, we dramatically change our outer world, say by suddenly changing our diet, we immediately create a situation which is in conflict with the old inner picture. Unless, or until, that inner

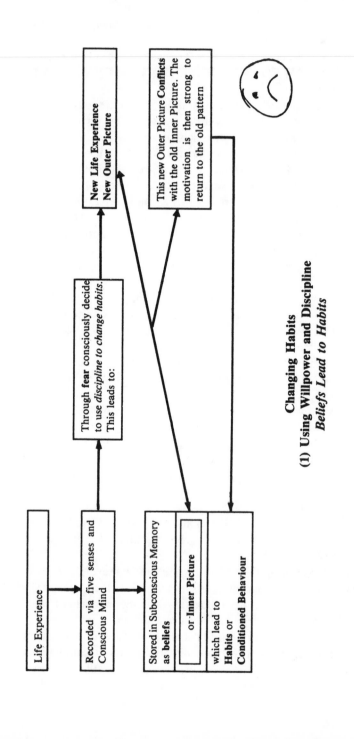

Changing Habits
(1) Using Willpower and Discipline
Beliefs Lead to Habits

picture is changed, there will be a constant urge to return to that old pattern or that old habit. Our mind will be working creatively against the new habit.

Now let's state the obvious:

> *To change your habits (the way you act)*
> *First, change your beliefs (the way you think).*

If we want to give up smoking, for example, there is no need to be concerned with how many cigarettes we are smoking a day. Be concerned with the beliefs.

Now, personally, I am very much aware of the fact that I am a non-smoker. If I suddenly found myself with a cigarette in my mouth, I would think I had gone crazy. I would be very strongly motivated to do something about it. I would want to put it out, quickly! So, if a smoker were to develop this same belief that I have, they would soon find themselves unable to endure the inner tension created if they did, in fact, continue to smoke. Be confident that, once that belief is established, whatever is needed to effect the change will be done. However, as with the goal of getting home, it is not enough just to have the mental picture; indeed some very real positive action may need to be taken. There may be a need to attend a Quit Smoking program, to seek out ways of replacing the needs smoking has been fulfilling, etc. But once that belief system is established — 'I am a non-smoker' — the motivation and creativity will work powerfully to fulfil the belief. You will do whatever it takes.

So, to take up a practical way of changing habits:

(1) Identify the Problem

Often this is obvious. You want to give up smoking, change diets, modify your behaviour. Concern for the problem requires the least emphasis in the process. The mind is goal-orientated. It is not so concerned with where we have been, what has been happening; it will respond best to the new direction, to where we want to go.

(2) Identify the Solution

This does require a good deal of emphasis. It necessitates the gaining of clarity and the setting of specific goals. We have already discussed this in some detail.

(3) Choose between 1 and 2

Here, do not overlook the fact that old habits, which we may currently judge to be 'bad', have almost certainly fulfilled very real needs. So why did we take up smoking? Peer pressure? Stress release? Comfort? At the time these were probably very real needs and, at that time, our resources for coping with those pressures were almost certainly limited. So, to take up smoking allowed us to survive that immediate crisis, but now we are stuck with an ongoing habit.

The question now is, do we still want to use that habit to meet those needs? Have our needs changed? Do we have other mechanisms for coping available? Is there a better way? Do we want to change and, if so, how?

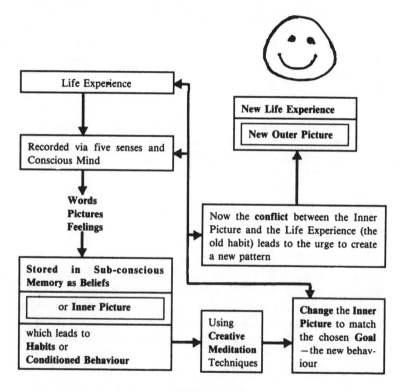

**Changing Habits
(2) Using Creative Thinking**

Using fear to invoke change seems to be non-productive. Understanding the real issues, being gentle with ourselves and with those around us, is far more likely to be effective.

Which is in our best interests — maintaining the old habit, or taking up on the solution? If we choose the solution then we are choosing to change. How then can we effect this change in the most reliable and painless way?

(4) Imprint the Choice

This is the mechanism of Creative Meditation and it uses the techniques of Affirmations, Imagery, and Feelings.

This process of Changing Habits can be represented diagramatically.

Now we see the joy of Creative Thinking. When we wish to change an old, undesirable habit, we can choose to first establish a new inner picture and believe in it. Then, all our inner creativity and resources will be mobilised to help us to match up our outer world action with the new inner picture. This is the way to change habits effectively and painlessly.

3 Creating Positive Emotions

This same process can be applied when we want to change our emotional responses, the way we feel or the nature of our relationships.

Consider here the impact of a traumatic emotional experience on our beliefs and our life. Imagine a young girl molested by her father. A frightening, puzzling experience causing all sorts of feelings that almost certainly cannot be shared with anyone else at that tender age. So what happens? This powerful experience registers with the subconscious. It is stored deep down inside, creating a powerful memory, one that the conscious mind may even choose to suppress from recall as being too painful. But, at that subconscious level, the incident indelibly remains, and with it could go a whole range of beliefs: Daddy can't be trusted; authority males can't be trusted; sex is unpleasant and frightening; what's wrong with me, anyway, that this thing happened; all men are ratbags. The possibilities go on.

Now, of course, the problem. We have a basic commitment to act in accordance with our beliefs if we are to judge ourselves sane.

Say the girl comes out of the experience with the subconscious belief that 'all men are ratbags'. She has a commitment to act in accordance with that belief. As a result, she will then be magnetically drawn to people and experiences that will reinforce that belief even if, consciously, it is a painful process. As the girl matures she is likely to be apparently inexplicably drawn to men who fulfil her expectations of being 'ratbags'. The need to experience peace of mind, to match our outer experiences with our inner beliefs, is so strong that we will often endure extreme hardships to do it. So, if we are negatively programmed, we are highly likely to experience life as a negative event.

Often, then, we see people who seem to pass from one life disaster to another, getting into deeper trouble on each occasion, when everyone around can see the problem and all seem powerless to help.

Why is this so? Even the person involved can make the conscious assessment that this is not right. 'I will learn by this last mistake. It won't happen again.' Then, Wham! Straight into the next similar disaster.

This compulsion to re-create childhood hurts makes a lot of sense when you understand the basic mechanism of the mind's function, the compulsion to act in accordance with our beliefs.

However, the news is not all bleak. In re-creating the same experience there comes the opportunity to resolve the old conflicts and gain a new degree of peace of mind—one that is satisfying on both the subconscious and the conscious level.

By facing the problems in our lives, understanding their nature and changing our attitudes to them, we *can* be freed from them. This is the process of Creating Positive Emotions.

Creating Positive Emotions

This four-step process is highly effective when all four steps are used in conjunction.

1   Meditate

Use simple, basic Health Meditation to allow the bulk of the 'mud' to settle; to let go of most of the old traumas, fears and conditioning. In this way you will regain your basic equilibrium and balance. This type of meditation also helps by developing the inner mobility and freedom that will enable you to make changes effectively.

2 Choose a new direction

Clarify your intended goals, your new attitude, feeling, belief, goal. These goals may well come out of Contemplation, Self Analysis, Insight Meditation, talking with friends or family, or they may come out of formal counselling. The idea is to define the area that needs to be changed and to establish the new pattern.

For example, if anger is the problem, if you react with anger as a habitual response, then how do you choose to react now? The answer may be, 'With love'. Then establish the need to react with love as the goal.

3 Imprint the new choice

Use Affirmations, Imagery and Feelings. (The details of how to do this are covered in the next chapter.)

4 Acknowledge and release old patterns—if and when they re-emerge

Steps 1 to 3 will remove the bulk of problems with great ease. It is not uncommon, however, for one or two major issues to present as real barriers to happiness.

Sometimes these issues will surface spontaneously in meditation, bringing with them a quite powerful emotional response. Quite commonly, in the meditative state, it is possible to review the old incident or current complex situation, and to feel the emotions that have gone with it. But now, in meditation, you may well understand it better, gain insight into the real issues involved and feel a sense of release in letting it go. This will never remove the memory of what happened—that is not intended. What it will do, with a good degree of certainty, is to take the intensity of the pain out of that memory or situation,and so make it far less of a negative influence on your life and behaviour.

Sometimes it seems appropriate to seek to understand and release old patterns through the more active and deliberate process of Contemplation or Insight Meditation. Some people can undertake this for themselves and set themselves specific questions or situations as the basis for their contemplation. Others find it a benefit and an asset to have a counsellor to support and guide them.

The more I experience of all this, the less I am impressed with cathartic means of emotional release and favour this gentler, more inward management of emotional trauma. In my experience, this is an effective way of overcoming such problems. It has very little risk attached to it, it does not open up issues that people are not ready to face or do not have the resources to face, and it still leaves the responsibility for the change with the person involved, not giving it to some 'whizz-bang' technique or therapist.

Creating Positive Emotions then involves releasing old issues and patterns through meditation and setting new goals, new directions, using the Imprinting Process. This is a gentle but powerful and effective way of making meaningful and lasting personal change.

The only limits are:

1   Your commitment to the old pattern

2   What you can accept as possible

3   Your commitment to persevere, your desire for change

Often people seem to think that they deserve to be punished, that they should suffer, that they are not worthy of being healed, of being happy, of experiencing well-being. There are creative ways of overcoming these common feelings, but, if they are overwhelming, apparent resignation and apathy will be evident. Of course, people experiencing these feelings, in fact, have a clear goal of suffering. If they were not suffering they would think they were crazy. While they are suffering at least they have that basic peace of mind provided by matching their experience with their beliefs. They are those unfortunate people who are never happy unless they are miserable!

This is quite a common condition. People afflicted by it often need to question their basic philosophy. Was the world as we know it created by a loving God? Were we born unhappy sinners destined for a life of sorrow? Or is this world a special place? Is to be born a wonderful gift? Are we destined for ultimate pefection? Dare we hope for contentment and well-being?

It seems so often we are conditioned to be average. We confuse being good at something with unfair advantage. Part of the joy of Insight Meditation is to come to understand our own strengths and weaknesses, as well as those of others, and to come to experience that the basic driving force in the Universe is a real and tangible force of Love.

Our natural state is pure and whole and loving. There is no doubt of that in my mind. Anything else is an artifact.

When we see clearly, when we drop off all that conditioning based on the false perception we have gathered over the years, then this is what we see. Every human being does have this pure and true inner core. We can all demonstrate it. Life provides us with the opportunity to experience this perfection here and now, and to use it for good. This is worth the struggle. This is the goal. It is worth doing whatever it takes, and the process certainly is fun!

Enjoy!

Chapter Ten

ACHIEVING YOUR GOALS: THE PRACTICALS

Understanding now the mind's tremendous potential to create or destroy our happiness, we can appreciate still better the three pathways of meditation. It is worth re-emphasising this to help that process of clarification and to build our confidence in what we are doing.

1 Health Meditation

Here we aim to still the intellectual mind. By doing so we enter a state of deep physiological rest which enables all our natural balancing and healing mechanisms to work at their best. To do so is relatively easy, beginning with the Relaxation Response and working steadily towards stilling the mind.

2 Insight Meditation

Here we aim to learn to be in the present moment, to develop presence of mind, to be aware of what is, what is real. This takes us clear of the conscious mind's fantasies of what was and what may be, and leaves us free to give one hundred percent attention to this moment. Doing so enables us to respond fully and appropriately to each and every moment, to be fully efficient, to be fully satisfied in each and every moment. To do so is a supreme achievement and marks the pinnacle of human development.

3 Creative Meditation

In this process, the aim is to use the power of the mind in a creative way. Utilising our knowledge of the mind we learn how to avoid being buffeted by our past conditioning with all its mixture of hopes and fears. We then come to recognise the power for good that the conscious mind clearly has and we learn how to use it to best effect. These, too, are skills that can be learned and practised. The essence lies in setting clear goals and then using techniques to achieve them.

So, having examined goal setting, let us now look at how to achieve those chosen goals using the techniques of Creative Meditation.

Imprinting

Imprinting is the conscious process which enables us to establish a chosen goal as a belief. This belief then acts as something that our mind will accept as a target to work creatively towards.

The aim of imprinting is to create a well-established inner picture, a new inner reality for our subconscious to work with. The reasoning is that this will stimulate all our inner resources to creatively produce this inner picture as an outer reality.

How affirmations work

Affirmations are short, accurate statements describing our goals. If, for example, we choose to be more positive in our approach generally, using an affirmation can establish that goal. Now, if we were to say something like, 'I hope to become a more positive person at some time in the future; maybe, with a little bit of luck, I possibly will', the mind is not going to be impressed at all. What a load of garbage to target on to! What is needed is a tight statement of the intention. Once this is well established in our subconscious, it will surface in any situation where being positive is an issue. This directive statement—this Affirmation—will then automatically and subconsciously direct our behaviour in the chosen direction. 'I am a positive person now' is, in fact, a tight statement of intention that will clearly direct the mind how to act. Once we have imprinted that statement, 'I am a positive person now', and established it as a subconscious belief, every time we are faced with a decision that needs to be made, a little voice inside will be saying, 'I am a positive person now'. To feel content with the decision we are about to make, to maintain our peace of mind and our sanity, we will have to make that decision in a manner which we can judge as being positive. So gently, effortlessly, like an automatic pilot, the affirmation will direct our behaviour towards fulfilling the goal.

However, when starting to use the Imprinting Process, the goal will not have been reached — yet. At this stage you are using the process to enlist the mind's magnificent resources in achieving the goal. Therefore, it is quite natural to expect an element of disbelief or untruth *when you begin.* You may believe you are quite a negative person when you commence this practice. That is all right — as a starting point. Imprinting is the process that can help you to change that. We are not lying to ourselves, but redirecting our attention. Now that we understand the way the mind works, we choose to establish a new belief, imprint it clearly and firmly enough, and expect the changes to take place — effectively and painlessly.

What affirmations to use?

There are books available with reams of standard affirmations, one for every occasion. I will include a few of my favourites as samples. However, it is best to use these merely as guides. Some may seem to be exactly tailored to your needs, but the best affirmations are those you create yourself, using your own knowledge, words and symbols. So, how is it done?

The three essentials of writing affirmations

Affirmations, to be effective, must be written:

> — in the first person,
> — in the present tense, and must be
> — *goal orientated.*

This is a personalised process, something we do for ourself, hence most Affirmations begin with 'I am' or 'I have', etc. Present time is the only time that the subconscious responds to, therefore Affirmations should indicate that the goal is already achieved or reached. The aim is to give the mind a target that it can lock on to — the target is the end goal, hence, 'I am a positive person *now*'.

Other guidelines for affirmations

1   Be positive

Indicate what is needed, not what is not. The mind is goal orientated, it locks on to targets. It needs a positive direction to aim for, not something to avoid. So, do not say 'I am not a negative person now' as an affirmation, but use 'I am a positive person now'.

2 Do not make comparisons

There is no need to say, 'I am as good an artist as little Johnny'. Your potential may be to be better, or it may be to be worse. Aim to develop affirmations that encourage the development of your full potential.

So little Freddy would benefit from an affirmation like: 'I draw confidently and accurately, with great style and enjoyment'.

3 Unless essential, do not specify a time for completion

As with comparisons, specifying time may slow you down or frustrate you. Part of the joy in using Affirmations is that they release the power of our Creative Subconscious and Inner Wisdom. The fact is that this part of our being has a wonderful talent for getting us in the right place at the right time — if we just leave it free to do so.

If you have observed your behaviour and find that you are regularly late, and you choose to change that, then certainly consider something like: 'I arrive on time for all appointments, content and at ease'.

4 Do be specific, accurate and accountable

The mind needs a specific target. The more precise the goal, the greater its clarity, and the more confident you can be of success. Remember, however, when setting those goals, the need to think like a dog, not like a duck, to keep an open mind and look for options. Once you have made a decision, however, then that is the time to become single-minded. As time goes on, do be prepared to obtain feedback, to be accountable, to assess your progress and make adjustments to your path when required.

5 Be realistic

You will be limited by what you believe is possible. It is normal to expect some reaction to using Affirmations. 'I am a positive person now', you say. 'No, you're not,' comes that little doubting echo. That is normal. The echo is the old belief having its say. If it were not there, there would be very little need to use the Affirmation in the first place. Remember that this process directs or redirects the mind's attention and mobilises all its power and creativity. This is a process for making change, for replacing one belief with another, as well as simply establishing a new belief or goal. So do not be surprised by the echo. As long as the Affirmation has more certainty, more expectation, more hope, more *oomph* than the echo, it will gradually replace it and soon become the guiding force.

However, you will need to stay within the bounds of what you can believe is reasonably possible. Do not aim for perfection first off! Be gentle with yourself and gradually set increasingly higher standards and goals.

This can be important with something like a major illness. Perhaps, at the beginning, someone just cannot see themselves fully recovering. If they could, then certainly it is a great thing to affirm, but perhaps it is enough to work on stabilising the condition first, to maintain the present position. Once this is achieved, the confidence will improve and perhaps then an ongoing goal can be set — say, reduction by half in the symptoms. Seeing this occur will allow the aim to be readjusted to take in the complete picture — an absence of illness.

6   Set ongoing goals

This follows on from what was just said. It is often interesting around the end of the football season to see the last few teams battling it out for a place in the finals. These teams put a great deal of concentrated, even inspired effort into playing well enough to win their last few matches and to gain a place in the final series. Not uncommonly, once this goal is achieved, they then relax, lose their competitive edge and get trounced in those finals. Their end goal was only to play in the finals. They did not set the ongoing goal of winning the final.

As you see yourself nearing completion of one goal, look for what comes next. Extend your planning and make new resolves.

7   Use Action Words and add a sense of excitement

The feeling that goes with an Affirmation has a lot to do with how quickly it will Imprint and be accepted by the subconscious. Affirmations, therefore, work better when said with zest and excitement. One way to do this is to add 'Wow!' on the end of them: 'I am a positive person now – Wow!' Saying 'Wow!' encapsulates that positive, expectant feeling. If 'Wow!' does not suit you, use another word or phrase from your own vocabulary to enliven your Affirmation.

Similarly, look for ways of expressing confidence, ease, naturalness and joy in all you aim for. Hence the words used earlier: 'I draw confidently and accurately, with great style and enjoyment'.

8 Be precise with the use of your words

Words used in Affirmations are definitely words of power. Pay great attention to how they might be interpreted. The most dramatic example I know of here was a friend who Affirmed a genuine need for ten thousand dollars. He got it all right – his father died and left him exactly $10,000 in his will! Coincidence? Quite likely, but it had a devastating effect on our friend because of the doubts it raised.

You can cover your bets by adding words like 'in a harmonious way'.

Similarly, watch the placement of words. 'I enjoy drawing confidently and accurately' may be interpreted literally so that in reality you still draw badly and do not enjoy it. Be as clear and precise as possible, consider all angles and choose your words wisely e.g. 'I draw confidently and accurately, with great style and enjoyment'.

Meditating and contemplating upon your choice of Affirmations before you use them is an excellent way to check their meaning and their validity – for you.

9 Keep a balance

Affirmations can have a profound effect upon your direction in life. Consider again the range of goals you are setting. Take heed of your physical, emotional, mental and spiritual needs and those of your family, friends and community. Affirmations are exciting tools to use. Aim to maintain that sense of balance.

Some sample Affirmations for personal development

These are some favourite Affirmations which can act as a guide for your own needs.

For health

'Every day in every way I am getting better and better'. This is one of the oldest and most famous Affirmations. It was first used by the Frenchman, Emile Coué. (See *Self-Mastery through Conscious Autosuggestion*, Allen and Unwin, 1984.) It remains an extremely powerful and effective tool for mobilising our inner drive towards better health.

For relationships

'I respond with Love now.'
'I greet this person with Love', (or, 'this day').

For attitudes

'I am a positive person now.'

For self-esteem

'I am worthy of being here.'
'I am worthy of being happy.'
'I am worthy of being loved.'
'My true nature is pure and one with the Divine.'
'God has a plan and a purpose for me. My thoughts and my actions are in tune with it now.'

On being able to change

'I can choose new beliefs (or habits), persevere, and make them a part of my nature.'
'My motives are pure and the decisions I make are appropriate to my needs.'
'I act on my decisions with perfect timing.'
'I persist until I succeed.'
'I remain·unattached to the results of my actions.'

Before discussing the finer practical details of how to actually use Imprinting combined with Affirmations, Imagery and Feelings, let us now look at how to develop Imagery.

The use of Creative Imagery

Imprinting is achieved through the use of words, pictures and feelings. Creative Imagery is the use of inner pictures to imprint a new goal on our subconscious and so to stimulate our motivation and creativity to achieve that goal.

In my experience about 75 per cent of people can readily form inner pictures. This is done by closing the eyes and imagining scenes as if you were watching an internal video screen. Of those who have difficulty, some are able to develop the skill by practising. As discussed previously, you can begin by looking at a scene or a photograph, then closing your eyes and trying to reconstruct it. Then move on to practise with images of scenes you are familiar with. With patient practice, most people can produce strong images if they choose to.

Note—the more complete the Imagery, the more readily it is accepted by the subconscious, and the more readily it imprints. So, as well as the pictures, it is useful to add sound, smell, touch and taste where appropriate. The more vivid, the more realistic the Images, the better.

Types of images

There are three classifications for the Images used in imprinting—Literal, Symbolic, and Abstract.

Literal Images

Here the aim is to see an image of the behaviour, event, or goal literally, the way you are aiming for it to happen. This type of imagery is very practical and can be applied in any situation where there is a clear understanding of the goal.

This approach is widely used in sport. We recently had a top golfer in our group who said he spent about half his practice time sitting in an armchair with his eyes closed! Mentally, he would practise his swing, making adjustments and perfecting it in his mind before going on to the fairway to put it into practice.

Similarly, if you have a very tangible goal like giving up smoking, creative imagery can be a great asset. Imagine yourself in situations where you used to smoke, only now see yourself calm and relaxed, not smoking, and feeling a sense of pride and achievement.

Combining this with an Affirmation such as, 'I am a happy, clean-mouthed non-smoker' virtually assures a change in the behaviour.

This technique also works well to change conditioned aversion responses like vomiting reflexly before having chemotherapy. Relaxing into the Relaxation Response and then practising the desired behaviour in your mind will change the conditioning, the belief, and allow for a new pattern to develop.

This inner rehearsal, in conjunction with simple meditation, also works well with many phobias. Say you suffer from arachnophobia (fear of spiders). To see a spider may cause extreme panic and immobilise you. However, at a time when that fear has not been strongly stirred, if you relax thoroughly and close your eyes, is it possible to think of a situation in which you could feel comfortable knowing there was a spider around? Perhaps it might be all right if you imagined the spider locked in a jar, in a house two streets away. You may be able to imagine that and not be jolted out of your relaxed state by the fear. So you practise staying calm and imagining the spider, gradually bringing it closer to your presence *only* as you feel comfortable. At any time you feel uneasy, use your mind to remove the spider and to reenter the relaxed state. If need be, you can always simply open your eyes and be assured of being in the comfort and security of your own room, free of spiders.

As you practise this you will go through a progression of steps. After a while perhaps it will be possible to imagine the spider out of the jar, still two blocks away. Then, as you feel comfortable with that, you can imagine it one block away, a few houses away, next door—making progress only as you are comfortable, bringing the spider closer into your field of experience. Perhaps then you can be comfortable imagining a spider on your verandah, in your furthest room, and finally on the wall opposite you. Then you will be able to start imagining yourself coming into a room, seeing a spider unexpectedly and not reacting with fear or panic, just calmly seeing the spider, recognising and acknowledging it, keeping out of its way and feeling calm and relaxed.

This process of using Creative Imagery to desensitise a fear or phobia can take some time. It may take many sessions before you can do it well, but it does work very effectively. Once you have desensitised yourself to the inner, imagined picture, then comes the real life test, to face the fear and test your reaction. People who have done this are consistently surprised by how well the method works.

The same technique is used for overcoming the chemotherapy response. Patients are taught to relax deeply, then to imagine going for the treatment. They imagine that they are really there — not that they are watching a video of themselves but that they are really there. In the car approaching the hospital. Parking. Going up the stairs, into the lift, into the waiting room. Into the treatment room. Having the injection. If at any stage the calm is lost, they back up, go back a step or two, let the nausea settle and regain their composure. They may only get to the car park in the first session. They are encouraged to finish each session when the calm has been restored so that they do not carry a bad feeling away from the session. At the next practice, they may get a little further, gradually reenacting the treatment until it can be imagined calmly and easily.

This process also works well for people who need repeated injections, and can be an excellent way of preparing for dentistry without anaesthetic when used in conjunction with pain management techniques.

It is also an extremely effective way of preparing for any new or challenging activity. So, if you need to speak in public and are concerned about it, sit down quietly, close your eyes, and relax. Then rehearse the whole event in your mind, building as complete an image of the meeting as you can, as if you really were there. If at any stage you feel apprehension, anxiety or fear welling up, leave the Imagery and return to the calm, relaxed feeling of simple, still meditation. You may need to consciously release tension from your stomach or other body areas. You may need to breathe more slowly and steadily to restore the calm. This comes more easily with practice. Having restored your equilibrium, recreate the scene, taking the calm into it with you. Each time you do this you will get further into the experience. Once you have rehearsed it several times you will be able to finish, feeling confident and assured, taking a pride in having done what needed to be done and having done it well.

This method of Mental Rehearsal using Creative Meditation is an extremely useful and practical technique.

The special case of pain control

Chapter Six in *You Can Conquer Cancer* (1984) discusses pain control at length. I have seen many people make significant reductions in the need for analgesics and some have been able to go through quite major procedures remaining calm and relaxed without anaesthetics.

Imagery is another useful aid in pain control. If you ever do experience a significant pain, this specific process is worth trying, in conjunction with the understanding and techniques offered in my other book.

Imagery for the relief of pain

1 Sit or lie in a symmetrical position and close your eyes.

2 Relax as completely as you can without giving this step too much attention. Do not try to force yourself to relax; do it as easily and as deeply as you can. If you have already established a practice of meditation, aim to recall the feeling of deep relaxation and to elicit the Relaxation Response.

3 Move your attention through the body, seeking out an area that feels different — an area that is painful, tight, under pressure, etc.

4 Be aware of where the sensation is in your body, for example the tummy. Be as specific as possible, e.g. close to the skin, deep in the abdomen, in the upper or lower region, etc. Where is it?

5 Be aware of its shape. Is it like a ball, a sphere, a rod? What is its shape?

6 Be aware of its size. Is it two centimetres across, or four centimetres by two by one? And so on. What is its size?

7 Be aware of its density. Does it feel heavy or light? Is it the same all the way through? What is its density?

8 What does it feel like? What is its surface texture? Is it soft and fuzzy, or hard and smooth? What does it feel like?

9 What colour is it? If this is vague, imagine what it might be like. What is its colour?

Having developed a good image of the pain in this way, there are then several options:

1 Repeated scanning:

Keep repeating the process of scanning the body, locating and examining the pain using the above guidelines. To aid this process, and particularly for someone in distress, you could ask a relative or friend to ask you questions based on the above points, e.g. Where is the pain located? Specifically? What size is it? and so on. You would answer the questions quietly to yourself.

This process is further enhanced if the support person breathes in time with the person in pain and talks in a quiet, slow and confident manner. They may need to relax themselves first and establish their own inner calm before beginning.

Once the pain is fully experienced in this manner, it will often simply fade away.

2 Internal relaxation:

Having developed a complete image of the pain, put your centre of attention inside that image and consciously relax it. Doing this may cause an initial increase in discomfort as you concentrate fully on the pain. There is no avoidance here. This is a process that will enable you to pass through the pain and become free of it.

Having already established a practice of Health Meditation, a familiarity with consciously relaxing your body will make this technique easier, however, it can work very well for beginners. Usually, as you relax the pain from the inside, it feels like a bubble bursting in slow motion as the outer shell of the pain breaks down and a wave of warmth and relaxation spreads from the inside out. This wave usually feels as though it extends out into the rest of the body, and feels very pleasant.

3 Triggering endorphins:

Sometimes while this process of concentrating upon a pain and releasing it is being practised, there can be a natural release of endorphins, the brain's opiate-like pain relievers.

This is the same effect experienced by many long-distance runners. Commonly, after eight or nine miles, the runners experience their 'second wind' or 'break the pain barrier', a stage that is accompanied by a powerful sense of euphoria. This is the body's natural mechanism for dealing with protracted pain and it brings profound relief. In fact, it often produces a deep sense of well-being.

Some people have learned how to trigger this response consciously and so top up their pain management.

4　*Talking to the pain:*

Some people find that they can talk to their pain. This may sound unusual at first, but sometimes an image of the pain arises spontaneously during this sort of imagery, and communication can be established with the person, animal or object that appears.

What is happening is that the Creative Subconscious is using an image to enable us to talk to our own Inner Wisdom. This often leads to an insight into the nature of the pain and to its resolution. So you could ask:

> *'Is it all right to talk to the pain?'*

If the answer is 'Yes', you could then ask all or any of:

> *'What is causing the pain?'*
> *'What is the pain's purpose?'*
> *'What is needed to make the pain go away?'*

Note: I do not use this method routinely myself, as I find I get better results with Repeated Scanning and Internal Relaxation, and triggering endorphins occasionally occurs naturally. However, this approach has been very effective for some people.

To conclude: This approach to pain control has no element of avoidance in it. It is a means by which the pain can be experienced as it is, free of fear or false imaginings. Commonly, when this is done, particularly in conjunction with the practice of Health Meditation, the pain can be experienced as a sensation which, while it may be unpleasant, is certainly free from distress.

This technique has great merit as, once established, it requires little energy to maintain it. The pain can be acknowledged and accepted, and life can carry on free from its effects.

Limitations of literal imagery

Literal images are often found wanting when you are faced with a complex situation and where your knowledge of the process required to achieve a given goal is unclear.

This is often the case in healing. Imagine a broken leg. The wonderful but complex process required to heal the break can certainly be influenced by our state of mind. However, trying to dictate literally to the body's repair system *how* it should heal the broken leg, would require a detailed knowledge of anatomy and physiology as well as an incredible sense of timing. The complexity of this process is beyond most, if not all, conscious minds.

To cater for this subtlety and complexity, these healing functions were placed under subconscious control. Up until recently, current medical thinking has been that there was no effective way of the conscious mind affecting these subconsciously controlled functions. Modern medicine is only just realising what ancient yogis and mystics have known all along. Quite definitely the conscious mind can be taught how to influence these subconscious functions. There are ample stories, well documented, of yogis slowing their metabolism sufficiently so that they can be locked in airtight containers or buried underground for days. Happily, there is also a good body of evidence showing that ordinary common people can achieve quite remarkable results also. Biofeedback has led the way in this field but one does not need sophisticated instruments to learn how to influence the body's healing directly. The Imprinting process does it 'just fine'! Creative Imagery in either the Symbolic or Abstract form is probably the most powerful tool for this purpose.

Symbolic imagery

> *Imagery establishes a link between the conscious intention and the subconscious function.*

This principle is a key one in understanding how healing can be encouraged and developed using the power of the mind. For healing to be influenced by the mind, a link must be made between the conscious desire for healing and the subconsciously controlled healing process. That this *can* be done heralds exciting advances in all areas of medicine. This potential has been recognised for years through the cunning use of the placebo. Now we have a technique that enables us to use and develop this power consciously. There is no need for an astute doctor to 'trick' his patients into getting well or into getting the best out of their treatment. That doctor can now join with the patients, enlist their help and resources, and ensure the best possible results. Not to do so is overlooking a major resource that I believe can often make the difference between success and failure.

Using symbols for the images allows the intention of the Imprinting to be established with the subconscious, without limiting the method.

One could imagine, therefore, a broken leg as being like a bridge in need of repair. The workmen would be seen as symbolic of the healing process. As the image of the bridge being repaired is built up in the mind, there would be the conscious knowing that this symbolises the leg repairing.

Specific symbolic imagery for cancer patients

To illustrate this process at work, let us examine the specific needs of imagery for cancer patients. These principles can be adapted to any illness or situation. I use this example because I have most experience in this area.

When selecting symbols for Imagery, it is best to use ones that come to you naturally. Usually, once the concept and principles are explained, people find that this occurs with little effort. Generally, it is not wise to use someone else's images for your needs, unless both arose spontaneously and happen to coincide. Many people find that the images spring effortlessly into their minds; others find that by contemplating their situation and needs, the images arise out of meditation.

For cancer then, there needs to be a series of images with particular properties. The cancer itself is the best place to start.

1   The image for the cancer needs to be of something that is weak and confused, disorganised and vulnerable.

It should be small in amount and have little power. This is a realistic view. Cancer cells *are* 'primitive', in the scientific sense of the word. That is, they have no useful function, and they do not have a mind of their own. Their only claim on our attention is that they get in the way and cause problems. They have none of the efficiency, organisation or beauty of a normal cell.

2   The Body Defences need to be seen as being organised and
purposeful, powerful and effective.

This, too, is a realistic view. The body's defence, the immune system,
is a truly wonderful self-regulating series of mechanisms. This defence
system has eliminated cancer from our body before, regularly. It has
an enormous potential. With Imagery, we have a way of encouraging
the system to use every bit of that potential.

3   Any treatment being used should be symbolised as being strong
and effective against the cancer.

It should be viewed as being gentle on the rest of the body, causing
either no side effects at all, or a minimum of side effects from which
the body can recover quickly.

4   The images used should be as vivid, clear and positive as possible.

. With practice, they will always get better. Use all the senses possible
in the imagery. Consider not only seeing the symbols, but, where
appropriate, hearing, touching, smelling and tasting them as well.

Having decided upon an image for each component, there is then
a need for developing a sequence of action and an overall image of
health.

The sequence of action

This symbolically represents how the cancer will be destroyed and
removed. It is the 'how' of how it will happen.

My experience here is that it is best to avoid images of violence
or flagrant aggression, unless these very strongly and spontaneously
present themselves. The images do need to be effective and complete,
but this can be achieved in a sympathetic manner. The cancer, after
all, is a part of the patient's body. To be imagining piranha fish
tearing at your insides, or World War Three being enacted as
symbolic of your body healing itself, seems to me to be unbalanced.

The range of images I have seen used successfully is enormous.
Some examples are:

The body as a factory, the cancer as dirt, the immune system as
the cleaners.
The arteries and veins as pipes, the cancer as blockages in the

pipes, the treatment and immune system as a highly efficient team of specialist plumbers.

Pacman as a symbol for the immune system's white blood cells is a very popular and good image.

The body as a beautiful garden, the cancer as a particular variety of weeds, the immune system as the gardener who digs out the weeds, takes them off for burning and remains vigilant for any that regrow.

The cancer as grapes, the immune system as vigorous, healthy birds that come in to eat the grapes.

Care must be taken that the symbols are accurate and complete. People using them are strongly advised to at least draw their sequence of action out on paper, explain it to a relative or friend or, preferably, to an experienced counsellor. This acts as a check to make sure that the symbols do, in fact, convey the full and accurate intention. It is very common for adjustments in the sequence to be useful and necessary.

The image of health

This second image used in the sequence provides an end goal of total health. This then is a separate image of what is being targeted for overall.

So, having done the specific cancer treatment sequence of action, patients are encouraged to generate an image of themselves in full health, feeling calm and relaxed, confident, and achieving all their chosen goals in life. Once imprinted, this very broad image will stimulate the inner resources to work creatively towards this goal of full health.

Often people use images in nature for this purpose. Running along the beach, or being out in the country, feeling good, happy, confident, full of life and joy.

This type of Imagery is a very good way to round off any meditation practice session.

Abstract images

More and more, I have been finding that generalised, more abstract images are easier for people to work with. These carry less risk of using negative images and are highly effective. I now recommend that people consider this type of imagery first and foremost if they want to use imagery at all. It does vary. Some people, especially those with a well-developed intellect and competitive nature, seem to thrive on the Symbolic imagery, but the more Abstract imagery seems to fit very easily and naturally with the overall approach to health based on meditation practice.

Abstract imagery relies on using simple, archetypal images that are very direct and are commonly interpreted in the same way by many people. Please note, this does not mean that there are no exceptions to these interpretations. You need to use only those images that you feel very comfortable with.

Two effective Abstract imagery sequences are *The Healing Journey* and *The Healing White Light*. Both of these are available on cassette. *The Healing Journey* also appears in *You Can Conquer Cancer* and in Chapter Six in a more detailed version.

The White Light Healing Meditation

This is a powerful imagery sequence which you will find rejuvenates and revitalises you and it is a wonderful way to catalyse self-healing and convey your love and healing wishes to others.

Once you are comfortably seated, let your eyes close gently . . . turn your thoughts inwards . . . remember that this is a time for healing . . .

Feel your body relaxing . . . feel the muscles becoming soft and loose . . . feel your weight begin to press down into your chair, your muscles relaxed . . . feel any tension releasing . . . feel yourself relaxing deeply . . . completely . . . more and more . . . deeper and deeper . . . letting go . . . feel it all through the body . . . feel it deeply . . . completely . . . it is a good feeling . . . a natural feeling . . . feel the letting go . . . feel it in the forehead particularly . . . feel the forehead smoothing out . . . feel it all through . . . more and more . . . deeper and deeper . . .letting go . . . completely . . . deeply . . . letting go . . . more and more . . . deeper and deeper . . . letting go . . . letting go . . . letting go . . .

Now become aware of your breathing . . . it is not important whether it be fast or slow — just become aware of your breathing, whether it is fast or slow . . . the breath moving in and out . . . and, as you do, imagine that you are breathing in a pure white vapour . . . so, with each breath in, see this pure white light moving down through your nostrils, down into your chest and filling it with a pure white light . . . and, as you breathe out, imagine that you are releasing a grey light, a grey vapour, that carries with it all the old, the worn, and the unwanted . . . as you breathe in again, imagine that you are breathing in the pure white light and bringing with it all that is pure, and fresh, and vital . . . breathing out and releasing the old, and the worn, and anything unwanted in your system . . . breathe it out and release it.

Now, while this is happening, you may choose to imagine that the white light is originating from your idea of the Divine . . . it emanates from the Divine . . . and, if you conceive the Divine to have a form, then see it in that shape and imagine the white light spreading from its heart . . . so, if it be an elderly, male figure, see this bright light spreading from that figure's heart . . . if it be from someone like Mother Mary, see the white light spreading forth from her heart . . . if it be some other form, see the white light spreading down towards you . . . and if, for you, the Divine is more abstract, perhaps it may suit you to see the focus, the centre of this light, as being like the sun and imagining the white light as streaming forth from the sun as representing the centre of the Divine, radiating out a pure white light in your direction . . . and so imagine that from that source the white light streams forth and, as you breathe in, it passes down through your nostrils, down into your chest, filling it with all that is pure, clean, vital, healthy, and whole . . . and, as you breathe out, release the grey, the old, the worn, and the unwanted . . . so that, with each new breath in, you bring, from the Divine, a pure white light that fills your chest and, as you breathe out, you release any old and worn energy . . . anything at all you want to be free of . . . and allow yourself to settle into a rhythm . . . breathing in the pure white light, seeing it streaming down into your chest, and breathing out the grey . . . in with the white and pure . . . out with the grey, the old, and the worn . . .

And, as you continue, feel the white light coming down steadily into your chest, and the strength of the light in your chest, growing stronger, and brighter, and purer, displacing any old and worn and grey areas, filling your whole chest with a pure white light . . . a symbol of wholeness, purity, vitality, and healing . . . you may be feeling the white light too, as a warmth, like a gentle warm liquid spreading through you . . . perhaps it even tingles a little as it goes

With each new breath, draw in more white light, till your chest feels like it is aglow, filled with this pure white light, so that it feels it is radiating pure white light . . . and, as you breathe in again, you feel the white light beginning to spill over, travelling down into your tummy . . . as you breathe out now, you can direct the white light, down into your tummy and, as you see the white light travelling down, feel it relaxing . . . feel it releasing . . . feel it healing . . . purifying . . . and feel the warm white light travelling down, relaxing, releasing . . . feel the warmth, the relaxation, the softness . . . releasing any old and worn energy . . . releasing any areas that are uncomfortable, painful . . . feel them being filled with the white light, with its comfort, releasing . . . and, as you breathe in now, draw in more pure white light from its source . . . see it travelling down into your chest . . . and, as you breathe out, radiate that white light down . . . down through your abdomen . . . down into your pelvis . . . releasing any tension . . . softening . . . bringing warmth . . . relaxation . . . deeply . . . breathing in more white light and seeing it travelling down now into your legs . . . down your thighs . . . softening . . . releasing . . . filling with a new strength . . . purity . . . bringing healing . . . and wholeness . . .

Breathing in more white light . . . seeing it passing down now, down into your calves . . . down into your feet . . . releasing any tension . . . releasing any old and worn areas . . . and bringing a new vitality . . . bringing healing . . . strength . . . so that now your legs, too, are filled with this pure, bright white light . . .

And, as you breathe in again, direct the white light now down your arms and feel the relaxation, the release . . . the softening, as your muscles loosen still more . . . right down . . . feel the light travelling right down into your fingers . . . feel them soft and loose . . . see them filled with the pure white light . . . symbol of purity . . . a feeling of natural vitality . . .

As you breathe in again, draw more of the pure white light from its source . . . see it filling your lungs . . . and now see it travelling up your neck . . . into your head . . . and, as it moves upwards, feel the muscles relaxing . . . feel them becoming soft and loose . . . feel any old areas being released . . . any worn areas . . . letting go . . . any diseased areas being freed, and replaced with a pure white light . . . symbol of new strength . . . of purity . . . of healing . . . of whole vitality . . .

So, now feel your whole body filled with this pure white light and, with each new breath in, draw more white light from its source . . . and see it filling your body with still more white light, so that your whole body is glowing intensely with the pure white light . . .

And, as you breathe in more, see the white light expanding out, beyond your body . . . to encapsulate you, like an egg . . . like a cocoon of bright, pure, white light . . . filling you with strength and vitality . . . feel it as whole . . . feel its unity . . . feel yourself to be at one with it . . . allow yourself to merge in the purity of the white light . . . feel its Divine Source moving through you . . . feel yourself to be at one with it . . . feel yourself at peace . . . be still . . . feel it all through . . . deeply . . . completely . . . all through . . . feel yourself at one . . . and be still . . .

As you feel its sense of wholeness through you, you may now like to direct that white light to someone you care for . . . to share that feeling with them . . . and so imagine them where you can, doing whatever . . . and imagine that, as you breathe in, the white light passes through you and radiates like a searchlight to the person you care for . . . and see them filled with its whiteness . . . see their body glowing white . . . and see them surrounded in a cocoon of pure white light . . . a symbol for purity . . . for wholeness . . . for healing . . . for renewed vitality . . .

And, as you breathe in, draw in more white light and radiate it to this person . . . seeing them filled with a new wholeness . . . a new sense of balance . . . purpose . . . seeing them whole and healthy . . . pure and vital . . . and share your experience with them . . . feel them, too, filled with the pure white light . . . and add your blessing . . .

Allow yourself to merge again with the feeling of purity and wholeness of the light . . . breathe in . . . breathe in more white light . . . see it streaming down from the Divine . . . pouring into you like a funnel . . . a funnel coming down through your nose and filling your body, and then radiating out . . . spreading out around you . . . and spreading off through your house . . . around wherever you are . . . see it filling your environment with the pure white light . . . see your room filling with the pure white light . . . and then it radiating further . . . filling your house . . . everyone in it . . . filling them with purity, wholeness, health, and vitality . . . feel your love flowing with it . . . feeling that warm, happy feeling going with it . . .

As you breathe in more, draw down more of this energy . . . as you breathe out, radiate it beyond the house . . . to the people around you . . . to the houses around you . . . feel it moving off, across the country . . .

Breathing in more white light . . . drawing it down, like a funnel . . . drawing it down from the Divine . . . through your body, and out across the land . . . spreading out, so that you can imagine the whole country bathed in this pure white light . . .

Breathing in more white light . . . breathing it out, and feeling it travelling right around the globe . . . wrapping the whole planet in a pure white light . . . and share your feeling of peace and unity with the whole planet . . . radiate that feeling out, and feel it travelling right around, so that the whole planet is held like a ball of pure white light . . .

As you breathe in more, feel that white light streaming down . . . feel yourself again merging with it . . . feel it entering every part of your being . . . feel yourself at one with its purity . . . at one with its peace . . . one with its healing . . . feel yourself at one with its vitality . . . and realise that that white light symbolises Love in action . . . allow yourself to merge into that feeling of Love, that Divine Love, streaming down and filling your whole being . . . feel it all through . . . feel its peace . . . be still . . . feel yourself merging with the stillness, to allow it to be all through you . . . completely . . . completely . . . be still . . .

Again, let us emphasise that the purpose of these Imagery Exercises is to establish a link between the conscious desire for physical changes and the subconscious mechanisms which control those physical processes. For success, these exercises rely on establishing a rapport, a link, between mind and body. Once this link is established, we are in a very creative and powerful position.

The Radiant Light Meditation

Another highly effective way of developing and strengthening this link is the *Radiant Light Sequence* also described in *You Can Conquer Cancer*. For completeness, it is reproduced here in full.

To begin, allow yourself at least thirty minutes. Visualisation can be done in any position, but I find this one works best if you lie down on a hard surface. The floor is ideal. Choose a carpeted area, or place a blanket underneath yourself to begin with. Lie flat on your back, hands loosely by your sides. Legs should be out straight, just comfortably apart, and the feet allowed to flop loosely outwards. Now place all your attention on just one big toe. Form an image of it in your mind and travel through it, looking closely at each part, relaxing it as you go and feeling that relaxation. Travel around the skin, under the nail, through the joints, tendons, ligaments and muscles. You will find you can see it all quite clearly and produce a profound feeling of relaxation in it. As you do so you will notice it becomes a little warmer. It may tingle a little. Gradually you then build up the image of a glowing white light suffusing it all. It is as if that toe was a light globe with a dimmer switch. You turn on that switch and gradually increase the light until the toe is full of vibrant white light. You will find it feels marvellous. When you do it well, you will be thinking of nothing else, just experiencing the vibrance of it all.

In effect you are using the five-step active meditation process with your own body as the focus of attention. You concentrate on your big toe, actively meditate upon it being relaxed, contemplate it, and while it is filled with vibrant white light, feel unified with it. It may sound strange to feel unified with your own toe, and with your whole body as you extend the process, but it is not. In this state of true unity and true balance lie harmony, healing and health. If you hold this feeling it has very positive effects.

So, begin with one toe. Then move to the next, and so on, until the whole foot is 'lit up'. You may find that at the first session, doing one foot takes all your time. That's fine. Next session you will find that you can recapture the feeling in that foot more easily and so can start with the next foot. At each session work on more areas until you can capture the feeling throughout the body. It is the feeling of relaxation, lightness and vitality that is the main thing. When you can do it well, you will have a means to relax yourself deeply and revitalise yourself amazingly. Practising this technique regularly, once a day for a few weeks, will produce a new dimension in body awareness and relaxation.

The clarity of visualisation of the different body parts is not so important. Obviously, someone with detailed anatomical knowledge will be able to build up a more detailed image than others. The important thing is to feel that close contact and awareness of each part of your body. So, in a large complex area such as the abdomen, you feel as if your mind is moving through the whole area. You feel the deep sense of relaxation and then the glow.

When it comes to areas affected by disease, just do the same thing. No effort or striving, just feel your mind moving through the area, relaxing it and letting the light build up to the same level as in the rest of your body. This produces a feeling of uniformity throughout the body – a vital, healthy uniformity, and it promotes the healing response.

Sometimes, relaxing areas affected by disease causes some initial discomfort. This is because we often impose tension in the region around them as a defence mechanism. These exercises relax that tension and often produce sensations of temporary discomfort, occasionally tingling, even brief muscle spasms or jerks. Be assured, this soon gives way to a feeling of warmth and ease and that this technique is also very helpful for pain control. *Note* the similarities of this exercise with the one described for pain control earlier in this chapter.

The regular practice of this technique develops a powerful link between mind and body. Combining this link with the abstract image of a pure white light transmits an abstract image of health, vitality, purity, strength and healing from the body to the mind.

When doing the exercise there should be an attitude of gentle strength, a quiet confidence that using this method will bring vitality, replenishment and health. As you practise it more, it can be completed very quickly. So, at times of flagging energy, you can just pause to recapture that feeling of light through the body and experience a rapid revitalisation. At other times, when there is a need for healing, you can spend longer periods practising the technique and so, subtly but powerfully, encourage and direct the natural healing mechanisms to work at their full potential.

The practice of Creative Meditation

To complete this section, let us consider a few practical details.

1 Why use it?

Creative meditation is ideal when you want to:

  (i)   Break free of past conditioning
  (ii) Change unwanted habits

(iii)   Set and achieve chosen goals

(iv)   Get the best out of the power of the mind and its ability to potentiate everything you do

(v)   Use the conscious mind to influence bodily functions such as pain control, healing, and athletic performance

2   *How to use it*

The process involves setting clear goals and imprinting them on to the subconscious.

Setting goals can and should involve the intellect, intuition and Inner Wisdom.

Imprinting relies on Affirmations, Imagery and Feelings, to establish a consciously chosen goal as a subconsciously anchored belief. This belief will then act as a target which the Creative Subconscious will do all possible to direct us towards.

3   *How often to use Imprinting*

Affirmations are best said with positive expectation, with power, confidence, and good feeling. If you can do this immediately, you will only need to repeat them for a minute or two a few times a day and they will soon become established. When you have a more challenging belief to establish, you will need to practise more often and for longer periods.

Imagery to go with Affirmations is used similarly—the time depending on the ease and clarity of using the image. Abstract Imagery can be used for longer times, the White Light Imagery, for instance, can easily occupy thirty to sixty minutes. Abstract Imagery makes an excellent prelude to Health Meditation.

4   *How to use the Imprinting process*

Imprinting is most successful when there is a close connection between the conscious and the subconscious. This is naturally so when we are in that reverie state just after awaking and just on going to sleep. This, then, is an excellent time to practise Affirmations and Imagery.

Also, singing or joking with Affirmations loosens the power of the conscious mind and its conditioned responses, and so facilitates the Imprinting process. Making up jingles for your Affirmations, and singing them out loud, therefore can be useful.

Looking directly into your eyes in a mirror and saying your Affirmations out loud with power and conviction is extremely effective if you can do it.

Best of all is to combine Imprinting with Health Meditation. The meditation provides a poise and balance and has a stabilising effect on the whole process.

A good sequence then is:

1. Sit in a slightly uncomfortable, symmetrical position.
2. Relax physically, inducing the Relaxation Response wherever possible.
3. Then begin the Imprinting process.

You can use Affirmations, Imagery and Feelings as a combined approach. This is the most direct and effective way. Sometimes it may seem more appropriate to use Affirmations or Imagery on their own. This may be when an Affirmation is being used to change an undesired state of mind of long standing. Beginning with, say, 'I am worthy of love now', may be best done as an Affirmation at first, moving on to adding Images once some confidence in the accuracy and reality of the Affirmation is established. Similarly, many healing situations appear to respond well to the direct use of Imagery.

5 Always practise simple Health Meditation in conjunction with Creative meditation.

The equilibrium so provided has a great balancing effect and provides for safety in using these extremely powerful and creative techniques.

6 Reinforce your positive approach

Do this using the principles already elaborated on in Chapter Three.

7 Then move on

Preferably move on from using any active Creative Meditation technique into the quieter stillness of Health Meditation.

8 Be prepared for new qualities in your Meditation

As time goes on, your practice of Creative Meditation will develop and your quality of health Meditation will improve. You may discover that this leads to your feeling in much better tune with your life and the world around you. You will move steadily into a better experience of current time. You may well find that there is then less need to practise Creative Meditation, that the process of goal setting and achievement begins to flow naturally and easily, and powerfully, with your passage through life.

CONCLUSION

So our traveller's guide comes to an end. The time to begin the practice is here. In meditation, with all its techniques and benefits, there is nothing as important as a commitment to regular practice. The book is intended to give an idea of the scope of meditation and to provide the confidence and motivation to begin or to strengthen your practice. It is for you to continue the journey.

We have covered many possibilities, many ways of travelling up the mountain towards that peak experience. It is a bit like writing a book on driving when some people will want to drive their car on easy suburban roads, others will want to work in a truck, and still others take on a Formula One racing car.

Remember that there are many paths up the mountain and that wherever you are coming from, wherever you are going, this journey is one that leads steadily to better health on all levels. Meditation is a journey of inner discovery. The grand adventure. The opportunity to get to know yourself better, the opportunity to find harmony and health in body, mind and spirit.

Recommendation on how to begin

Where to begin? I recommend that you start with *Integral Meditation*.

1 *Learn the Progressive Muscle Relaxation*

(The details are in Chapter Three.) This technique will help you to experience the Relaxation Response.

2 *As you practise it, concentrate on the feeling of relaxation*

As you feel your body relaxing progressively, allow that feeling to be all through you, go with it, simply settle into stillness.

3   *Maintain a passive approach*

There is no need to make something happen. Likewise, resist the temptation to assess your progress. These two ineffective attitudes are the greatest barriers to satisfying meditation. Adopt an attitude of gentle, positive expectancy and be prepared to accept and enjoy whatever happens.

4   *As your practice develops, simplify the technique*

Prune and refine it, working easily towards being able to use the Direct Method — towards being able to just sit and let stillness happen, simply, easily, directly.

5   *Be prepared for ups and downs, good days and bad days*

Practise in more uncomfortable and more challenging situations. As you progress, your skills will improve and you will soon be experiencing the benefits.

6   *If at any stage you experience overwhelming frustrations with the method, experiment with other approaches*

Use a secondary focus so that you have something else to fix your concentration upon. You almost certainly will benefit from practising at being the impartial observer. (Details of these techniques were outlined in Chapter Six.)

Remember that as soon as you can elicit the Relaxation Response, major health benefits will begin to flow. So merely by being able to sit still, to relax physically and to let the mind coast for a while, is a sure sign of major progress. As time goes on, deeper benefits will flow, easily and naturally.

Once you have established a routine of simple Integral Meditation and have experienced the balance and poise it brings, you may well want to find out more about yourself and the life you are living. Insight Meditation provides the opportunity to do that, and its principles were outlined in Chapter Seven.

You may also choose to use the creative power of your mind by adopting the principles and techniques of Creative Meditation. (The details were in Chapters Eight, Nine and Ten.)

Health Meditation

The overall conclusion is that Health Meditation, with its ideal technique being Integral Meditation, provides an excellent means of regaining balance. Health is a state of balance. This is a dynamic, active and efficient state, and Integral Meditation is a life skill that has a part in every person's life.

Creative Meditation

Creative Meditation can help us to function more efficiently and effectively in the world we know. It helps us to set specific goals and to achieve them. It is particularly useful if our life is beset by past conditioning and limited by negative attitudes. Creative Meditation teaches us how to set a clear, positive course in life.

Insight Meditation

Insight Meditation teaches us to concentrate and to observe. It helps us to be aware of what is real, to be mindful, to give full attention to this moment now. To be here now.

Insight Meditation can also lead to major insights that will transform our experience of life. In fact, this is so with any form of Meditation. If we were to use only the power of the mind, we would always be confronted by the limitations of the mind. If we use meditation as well, however, at any moment we may find ourselves at the top of the mountain, experiencing the wonder of the view, experiencing the wonder of contact with the profound stillness that lies within us all. It is a delightful mystery that within this stillness lie all the answers we have been seeking.

To experience the profundity of that stillness is to be transformed. Life will begin to flow with grace and ease. A sense of order, appropriateness and joy will mark all aspects of life as you experience it. Coincidences will cease to be — the Law of Synchronicity will become a delightful feature of life. You will find yourself increasingly to be in the right place at the right time. You will experience life as the meaningful pleasure it is meant to be.

It is a privilege to have been able to write this book and to share these pages with you. May you enjoy every moment of your journey. May Peace go with you.

THIS BOOK
ATTEMPTS TO PUT INTO WORDS
THAT WHICH IS BEYOND EXPRESSION

ITS TRUTH IS TO BE FOUND
IN THE REALMS
OF THE PRACTICE
AND THE PERSONAL EXPERIENCE
OF
MEDITATION

IF YOU ARE SERIOUS ABOUT
LEARNING TO MEDITATE,
YOU MUST PRACTISE
REGULARLY

ENJOY IT!

TWO-CORRELATE GRAPH OF ALTERED STATES OF CONSCIOUSNESS

This graph represents changes in basal skin resistance as a measure of physical relaxation (moving to the right represents an increasing level of physical relaxation) and electrical brain activity as a measure of mental relaxation, arousal or calm (moving down the graph represents an increasing level of relaxation and calm). It shows how panic is marked by physical and mental arousal and activity while deep meditation is marked by physical and mental relaxation and calm. Zen or Insight Meditation, however, is characterised by physical relaxation and mental activity.

TWO-CORRELATE GRAPH OF
ALTERED STATES OF CONSCIOUSNESS

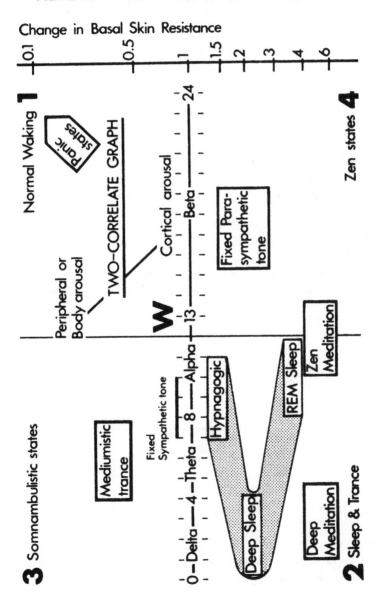

MIND MIRROR PATTERNS

Represented here are patterns recorded with the Mind Mirror. This is an EEG machine which is capable of recording the electrical activity of the left and right hemispheres of the brain, independently but simultaneously. No activity would be represented by two parallel lines down the centre of the panel.

Activity of the left hemisphere is marked by the left line moving left while activity of the right hemisphere is marked by the right line moving right.

The Mind Mirror is a powerful biofeedback tool developed by Maxwell Cade and his associates. The patterns are taken from his excellent book, *The Awakened Mind* written with Nora Coxhead, published by Wildwood House, Great Britain, 1979.

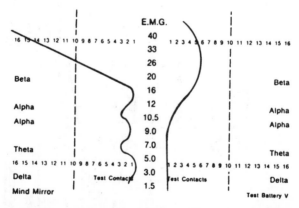

Diagram 1 **is the pattern of a not very still person. The left shows only beta activity, the alarm reaction of the sympathetic nervous system, which inhibits the activity of the right hemisphere.**

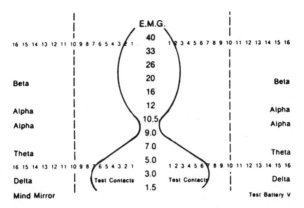

Diagram 2 shows a very calm person. Beta represents the alarm aspect of mental activity, while complex thought need not be accompanied by any beta activity whatsoever. A calm person may be very alert, directing his mental content as he wishes, and yet show only a small response in the beta range.

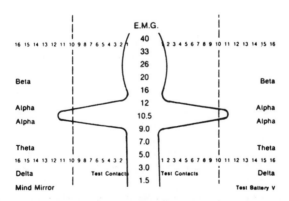

Diagram 3 Nothing but alpha, the pattern of the reverie state characterized by rapid, changeable, dreamlike images. Sometimes a subject may slip toward sleep instead of meditation, in which case only alpha will be present.

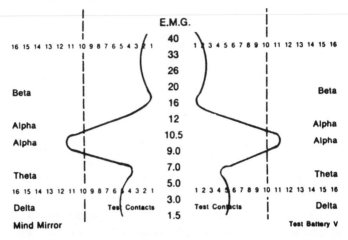

Diagram 4 is the pattern of a meditator with his eyes shut. Note the symmetry of the patterns, which becomes permanent once the initial difficulties, if any, of beginning meditation are overcome. The dominant frequency of the alpha peak becomes lower during meditation and is also a very approximate indication of how long meditation (or stillness) has been practised.

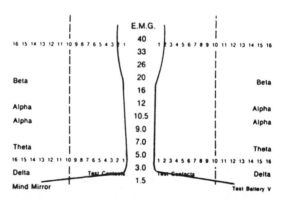

Diagram 5 At extremely deep levels of physical relaxation, both alpha and the theta have disappeared and only delta remains. This is not a sleep state, however; the difference of palmar skin resistance shows this, being around 80 per cent change, whereas in nondreaming sleep, the skin resistance change would be no more than 50 per cent.

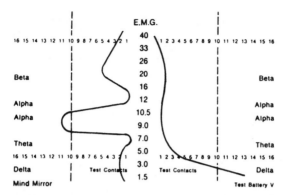

Diagram 6 We believe that this pattern graphically demonstrates what is meant by Jung's transcendent function—the ability to use the two halves of the cortex appropriately and independently. A healer we tested often shows this pattern when with a patient.

RECOMMENDED READING AND LISTENING

BOOKS

Books provide a wonderful, ongoing reinforcement and inspiration for your practice. Here is a collection of books that I value, those marked with an * being favourites.

Meditation

Al Chung-Liang Huang, *Embrace Tiger, Return to Mountain*, Moab, Utah, Real People's Press, 1979.

The essence of T'ai Chi, lovingly and exuberantly presented by a modern master.

Arya, R.A., *Superconscious Meditation*, Honesdale, Pennsylvania, Himalayan International Institute of Yoga, Science and Philosophy of the U.S.A., 1977

Meditation manual based on traditional Yoga texts, presenting a good range of specific techniques.

Arya, U., *Meditation and the Art of Dying*, Honesdale, Pennsylvania, Himalayan International Institute of Yoga Science and Philosophy of the U.S.A., 1979.

Combination of ancient Indian Wisdom and Philosophy and modern Western understandings – examines who we are and what is the meaning of life and death.

Bailey, A., *From Intellect to Intuition*, New York, Lucis Publishing Company, 1970.

The five stages of concentration, meditation, contemplation, illumination, inspiration explained. A means of seeking a direct spiritual reality. One of a series of valuable esoteric books; not easy to comprehend at first.

Bailey, A., *Letters on Occult Meditation*, New York, Lucis Publishing Company, 1970.

Explains mental techniques aimed at achieving specific results – either intense mental activity or stillness.

* Benson, H., *Beyond the Relaxation Response*, London, Collins, 1984.
Dr. Benson is a Harvard cardiologist. He travelled to Nepal to study Buddhist meditators and evaluate the physiological changes they can induce. He introduces the 'Faith Factor', as making the greatest difference.

Benson, H., *The Relaxation Response*, London, Collins, 1975.
Examines the effects of stress on our bodies, the use of meditation through the ages and scientific validation of its effects. Focusses on the benefits of meditation for heart patients.

Besant, A., *Esoteric Christianity*, Adyar, Madras, The Theosophical Publishing House, 1901.
A mystical examination of the essence of Christianity.

* Brunton, P., *The Hidden Teaching Beyond Yoga*, York Beach, Maine, Weiser, 1941.
One of Paul Brunton's many excellent books, all worth reading. This one examines the difference between feeling or believing, and knowing, and how to make the transition. Dwells on the great question, Who Am I?

* Cade, C. and Coxhead, N., *The Awakened Mind*, Hounslow, Middlesex, Wildwood House, 1979.
An excellent pioneering text in biofeedback and the scientific investigation of meditation with EEGs.

Chogyam, Trungpa, *Meditation in Action*, California, Shambhala, 1969.
An excellent introduction to the practical approach to meditation of the ancient Tibetan Buddhist tradition, given in a very readable modern style.

* Clynes, M., *Sentics — The Touch of the Emotions*, Garden City, New York, Anchor Press Doubleday, 1978.
A revolution in understanding how we experience and communicate emotion, with a practical meditative method of clearing, stabilising and enhancing emotional responses.

Drury, N. (ed.), *Inner Health*, Sydney, Harper & Row, 1985.
Health benefits of relaxation, meditation and visualisation, with one chapter by Ian Gawler.

Gawler, I., *You Can Conquer Cancer*, Melbourne, Hill of Content, 1984, Thorsons, Wellingborough U.K. and New York U.S.A., 1986, and as *Ein Signal der Seele?*, Peter Erd, Munich, West Germany, 1985.
Ian relates the methods he and Gayle used to overcome his own cancer and as subsequently translated into their cancer self-help and prevention program. Presents a practical approach to living well, based on meditation, positive attitudes and good food. This is a basic philosophy to live by which has been taken up by many non-cancer patients interested in well-being and the joy of life.

Geshe, R. and Geshe, D., *Advice from a Spiritual Friend*, London, Wisdom Publications, 1977.
Shows how, by gradually changing our attitudes to ourselves and others, we can, quite literally, learn to be happy and content in any situation.

Focusses on loving kindness, compassion and wisdom.

* Goldstein, J., *The Experience of Insight*, U.S.A., Shambhala, 1976.
An excellent guide to Buddhist meditation techniques and philosophies as given at a 30-day retreat. This is the Vipassana style of meditation.

Griffiths, B., *Return to the Centre*, Collins Paperbacks, 1976.
A series of insightful essays or meditations on the Christian faith from this inspiring Benedictine monk living in a South Indian ashram.

Humphreys, C., *Zen Buddhism*, London, Unwin, 1949.
An excellent presentation of Zen by the man who is renowned as probably the West's greatest exponent of Buddhism. One of his many worthwhile books.

Le Shan, L., *How to Meditate*, New York, Bantam, 1974.
A famous psychotherapist's simple, straightforward approach to the many paths into meditation.

Long, M.F., *Growing Into Light*, Marina Del Rey, California, de Vorss,1955.
One of Long's excellent books on the beliefs of the ancient Hunas people of Hawaii. Examines the traditional use of the spiritual and of mind power.

* Mason, L.J., *Guide to Stress Reduction*, Culver City, California Peace Press, 1986.
An excellent guide to many relaxation and meditation techniques, presented clearly and concisely.

* McDonald, K., *How to Meditate*, London, Wisdom Publications, 1984.
Probably the best introduction to the many useful meditation practices of Tibetan Buddhism by a very lucid, California-born, Buddhist nun.

McKinnon, P., *In Stillness Conquer Fear*, Blackburn, Victoria, Dove Communications, 1983.
Excellent account from an agrophobic who overcame her fear with meditation under the guidance of the late Dr Ainslie Meares.

Meares, A., *Cancer, Another Way*, Melbourne, Hill of Content, 1977.
Zen style sharing of a meditative approach to cancer.

Meares, A., *From the Quiet Place*, Melbourne, Hill of Content, 1976.
Reflections in Zen style, suitable for healing meditation.

* Meares, A., *Prayer and Beyond*, Melbourne, Hill of Content, 1981.
Marks the steadily deepening spiritual insights that came to Dr Meares through his own practice of meditation and his work with many people gaining from meditation.

* Meares, A., *Relief Without Drugs: The Self-Management of Tension, Anxiety and Pain*, London, Collins/Fontana, 1970.
A landmark book; a classic on meditation for personal healing.

Meares, A., *Thoughts*, Melbourne, Hill of Content, 1980.
Dr Meares' response to the world around him, Zen style. Good for contemplation, meditation.

Meares, A., *A Way of Doctoring*, Melbourne, Hill of Content, 1981.

A look at doctor/patient relations, silent communication skills, the value of meditation for therapist and patient.

* Meares, A., *The Wealth Within*, Melbourne, Hill of Content, 1978.

Here Dr Ainslie Meares, psychiatrist, describes in detail his simple yet profound approach to meditation, which he calls Mental Ataraxis.

Muktananda, *Meditate*, Melbourne, Siddha Yoga Foundation.

The guru of Siddha Yogi shares specific introductory techniques to meditation and the philosophy that goes with them.

Ramacharaka, M., *Hatha Yoga*, London, Fowler, 1960.

A landmark introduction to the basic tenets of Yoga, wonderfully presented by this practical and erudite Indian Yogi. One of an excellent series by this author.

* Ramacharaka, M., *The Hindu-Yogi Science of Breath*. 23rd Edition, Romford, Essex, L.N. Fowler, 1960.

Looks at the importance of correct breathing in the practice of yoga and how to benefit from it in everyday life and especially in conjunction with meditation. An excellent self-help guide.

Rozman, D., *Meditation for Children*, California, U.S.A, Celestial Arts, 1976.

A simple guide for teaching children to meditate.

Satyananda, *Yogasanas, Pranayama, Mudras, Bandbas*, Melbourne, Diamond Press, 1969.

An excellent, detailed introduction to the practice of Yoga by the founder of the International Fellowship Movement. Particularly useful for its section of Yoga breathing exercises – pranayama.

Segesman, M., *Wings of Power*, Melbourne, Hill of Content, 1973.

The techniques practised by a master of traditional yogic principles, applied in a readily accessible, Western style.

Steiner, R., *Knowledge of the Higher Worlds and Its Attainment*, London, Anthroposophic Press, 1947.

Introduction to Esoteric Meditation techniques and beliefs aimed at an understanding of the soul and superconscious.

Suzuki, Dr., *Zen Mind, Beginners Mind*, John Weatherhill, Japan, 1970.

Puts the basically non-intellectual Zen approach into an approachable form – the art of being here now. A classic on Zen meditation.

* Thick Nhat Hanh., *The Miracle of Mindfulness*. Boston, Beacon Press, 1976.

Vietnamese Zen master's masterful presentation on the nature of Zen, complete with many practical suggestions and exercises. Excellent book.

Vjayadev, Yogendra *Love as a Way*, Queensland, Warwick Centre Publications, 1982.

A yogi of traditional Indian background, who has studied widely in the

West, presents his answers towards helping individuals to rise to a full expression of love.

Yesudian, S. and Haich, E., *Raja Yoga*, Sydney, Unwin Paperbacks, 1980.
The authors describe the relevance of yoga — the conscious development of mind, soul and body — for our times. Raja yoga is a culmination of all forms of yoga, blending the philosophies of East and West.

Creative Meditation/Positive Thinking

Bach, R., *Jonathan Livingstone Seagull*, Sydney, Pan, 1973.
An inspirational fantasy.

Bandler, R. and Grinder, J., *Frogs into Princes*. Moab, Utah, Real People Press, 1979.
One of the basic texts explaining Neuro-Linguistic Programming, a very effective and simple way of creating a positive experience of life.

* Capra, F., *The Tao of Physics*, London, Fontana, 1983.
A powerful examination of the similarities between the current physics and the ancient wisdom of the sages.

Corsini, R. et al., *Current Psychotherapies: 3rd Edition*, Hasca, Illinois, F.E. Peacock Publishers, 1984.
A comprehensive and readable review of the many current psychotherapies.

* Cousins, N., *Anatomy of an Illness as Perceived by the Patient*, Sydney, Bantam, 1981.
Personal testimony of the united efforts of a patient and physician to overcome the effects of a crippling condition, mainly through the use of positive attitudes and Vitamin C. Cousins examines the role of the placebo effect and laughter in this excellent, readable book.

Bono de, E., *The Use of Lateral Thinking*, Ringwood, Victoria, Penguin, 1971.
One of the author's best of many books on ways of developing creative thinking.

Dyer, W., *Your Erroneous Zones*, New York, Avon, 1976.
Good practical advice on how to improve self-esteem and take control of your own life.

Ellis, A. and Harper, R., *A New Guide to Rational Living*, California, Wiltshire Book Co., 1961.
A very readable guide to self-evaluation and personal development.

Frankl, V., *Man's Search for Meaning*, New York, Pocket Books, 1963.
The major book of this psychiatrist, survivor of Auschwitz and originator of Logotherapy or Existential Analysis.

* Glasser, W., *Positive Addiction*, Sydney, Harper & Row, 1985.
The author urges readers to gain strength and self-esteem through positive addictions rather than negative ones such as smoking and drugs. He

recommends running and meditation to help us achieve a better quality of life.

* Harrison, J., *Love your Disease — It's Keeping you Healthy*, Angus & Robertson, Sydney and London, 1984.

A challenging book that explores the psychological needs for illness — how illness is often our best way of coping, why we often need to be sick and how we can choose to be healthy.

Hutschnecker, A., *The Will to Live*. New York, Simon & Schuster, 1951.

Shows how to avoid illness by understanding the emotional disturbances that can cause it. Presents a simple and effective plan for healthier, more secure living.

* Jampolsky, G.G., *Love is Letting Go of Fear*, Sydney, Bantam, 1981.

This is a book about self-fulfilment through giving. By transforming our own outlook on life, we can change how we perceive the world, the people in it and, finally, ourselves.

Le Shan, L., *You Can Fight for Your Life*, Wellingborough, England, Thorsons, 1977.

Offers insight into why some individuals get cancer and others do not, and gives examples of those who have been able to fight against the disease.

* Levine, S., *Who Dies? An Investigation of Conscious Living and Conscious Dying*, Garden City, New York, Anchor Press/Doubleday, 1982.

A very positive book which gives fresh insights into the process of living and dying. Levine believes that by being fully open to each moment of life we are preparing for death. Includes meditations on pain control and dying.

Maltz, M., *Psycho-Cybernetics*, Sydney, Bantam, 1978.

Psycho-Cybernetics concerns directing our mind to a positive self-image, to fulfilment as a human being. The author guides us in steps to relaxation and self-acceptance.

Moody, R., *Life After Life*, Sydney, Bantam, 1976.

Stories of those who have been pronounced clinically dead but recovered and reported having experienced startlingly similar effects.

Murphett, H., *Sai Baba: Man of Miracles*, Maine, U.S.A., Samuel Weiser Inc., 1973.

Excellent introduction to the Indian Holy man, Satya Sai Baba, who has been compared with Christ and Buddha for his phenomenal powers and spiritual message.

Sandweiss, S. H., *Sai Baba, the Holy Man . . . and the Psychiatrist*, San Diego, California, Birth Day Publishing Co., 1975.

Sai Baba is an Indian spiritual leader who, it is claimed, has superhuman powers. Samuel Sandweiss describes his time in India with Sai Baba and relates his beliefs.

Shinn, F., *The Game of Life and How to Play it*, Marina del Rey, California, De Vorss, 1925.

The author sees success in life coming through positive thinking and trust in God. Good sections on affirmations.

Silva, J., *The Silva Mind Control Method*, New York, Pocket Books, 1977.
    The text that explains the famous Silva Mind Control program and elaborates on principles of creative visualisation.

* Simonton, O.C., *Getting Well Again*, Sydney, Bantam, 1978.
    Emphasises the power of positive thinking and visualisation in contributing to the better health of cancer patients. Quotes many patients' experiences and gives advice to families of patients.

* Simonton, S.M., *The Healing Family*, Sydney, Bantam, 1985.
    A must for patient and family. Most positive and practical approach to helping families come to terms with a major illness and to create the most favourable environments for recovery.

Wilber, K., *Quantum Questions*, Boulder, Colorado, Shambala Publications Inc., 1984.
    The mystical writings of the world's great physicists. What attracted these great scientists to a personal experience of mysticism?

Yogananda, P., *Autobiography of a Yogi*, Bombay, Jaico Publishing House, 1983.
    Classic autobiography of a great Hindu yogi.

Two gentle books to bend your thinking

* Bach, R., *Illusions*, London, Pan/Heinemann, 1978.
    The adventures of a reluctant Messiah and his contact with a man seeking to understand his own reality—a positive delight!

* Persig, R., *Zen and the Art of Motor Cycle Maintenance*, London, Corgi, 1974.
    The journey of a man in search of himself — full of insights into our most complexing contemporary dilemmas.